QUEBEC IN QUESTION

QUEBEC IN QUESTION

MARCEL RIOUX

TRANSLATED BY JAMES BOAKE

James Lorimer & Company, Publishers
Toronto 1978

Originally published as *La Question du Québec,* Paris: Editions Seghers, 1969.

ISBN 0-88862-190-6 cloth
      0-88862-191-4 paper

Cover design: Don Fernley
Photo of Marcel Rioux by J.R.M. Sauvé *(Le Jour)*

───────────────────────────────

Canadian Cataloguing in Publication Data

Rioux, Marcel, 1919-
Quebec in question

Translation of La question du Québec.

ISBN 0-88862-190-6 bd.   ISBN 0-88862-191-4 pa.

1. Quebec (Province) — History — Autonomy and independence movements. 2. Quebec (Province) — Politics and government. I. Title.

FC2925.9.S4R5613 1978   971.4   C78-001044-2
F1053.R5613 1978

───────────────────────────────

James Lorimer & Company, Publishers
Egerton Ryerson Memorial Building
35 Britain Street
Toronto

Printed and bound in Canada

7 6 5 4   85 86 87 88

Contents

Foreword

My people came from Brittany to settle in New France in the seventeenth century. I am one of the first of their descendants to leave the lower St. Lawrence and the Gaspé to live and work in the city. My ancestors — like those of most Quebeckers — remained for several generations in small rural parishes, trying to preserve the heritage of the old country while adapting to life in North America. At first they all lived on the Island of Orleans; later they spread to Trois-Pistoles and to several smaller communities; today they are scattered all over Quebec. What sort of life did my people lead? Briefly, their sole concern was to cling to the soil, to survive. The winter of our discontent has lasted a very long time. Barely ten years ago it began to thaw, and spring has brought with it two ancient dreams — liberty and independence.

In this book I look at some aspects of Quebec's culture and society. I am a professional sociologist, and sometimes I speak from a sociological point of view. Elsewhere, I speak as a Quebecker who desires the independence of his country.

No man can be a fence-sitter where the life and death of his country is concerned. There comes a time when he must take a public stand. In this little book I have had the opportunity of taking mine.

M.R.

Chapter 1
The Quebec Question

Over 400 years have passed since Jacques Cartier discovered Canada (1534), and it is almost four centuries ago that Champlain founded Quebec (1608). Why then is there, today more than ever, a "Quebec question"? We live in an age of globe-straddling superpowers, common markets, space conquest, and a worldwide communications network that grows more integrated every day. Is it not outrageously anachronistic to raise the problem of a people numbering only six million, who do not know the tragedies of war or the agonies of hunger, like the Vietnamese or the Biafrans, and who live quite comfortably in North America, a continent with political stability and a high standard of living? Let us admit from the start that the Quebec question has neither the tragic character of the Israeli question nor the disturbing magnitude of the Chinese question. It is nevertheless a question asked for such a long time that, paradoxically, it is flagrantly up to date. The questions raised by Quebec belong to the main stream of problems concerning contemporary decolonization and political confrontation. It is frequently said of French Canadians that they are the richest colonized people in the world. What is not perhaps sufficiently emphasized is that they are also, without a doubt, among the oldest colonized peoples in the world, if not *the* oldest. These two dubious distinctions seem to indicate that men do not grow used to slavery, however long their servitude, and that a high standard of living is not enough to make them forget their values, their dignity and their honour. Jacques Berque says of Quebeckers: "They call themselves a colonized people, not, as they believe, for once having been annexed to a foreign crown, but because their coexistence with the Other in an environment saturated with the Other creates, between them and the Other, a sociological distance which would be abolished if they could escape from this environment. For some years, under the menace of separatism, measures have been taken to reduce the discrimination they suffer within Canada. As a result they cling all the more tenaciously to their distinctive and original characteristics. Moreover, they are colonials inasmuch as their identity cannot be based on the folkloric and the residual, to which one would like to reduce them. Correlatively their demands, which can be expressed only partly in terms of economic exploitation, are based primarily upon the argument of depersonalization — the depersonalization of customs, styles and language. Where other social claims are concerned, French-Canadian demands in many cases give more weight to culture than to economics and, definitely, more to the symbol than to the reality."[1]

Professor Berque has not neglected the economic and political aspects of the domination to which Quebeckers are subjected, and which, at the most obvious level, determines their cultural alienation. He has, however, certainly put his finger on one of the most important aspects of the Quebec question, that which relates it to all the movements of "cultural confrontation" that have appeared recently all over the world. When Marshall McLuhan speaks of French Canadians as "hippies," he is talking about this aspect. From this point of view, the case of Quebec is but one example of many and may, just as more obviously pathetic cases do, interest those who want to understand human nature.

It is true that a universal consciousness is being born and that men everywhere share the same hopes and fears regarding the effects of expanding economic and technological patterns of change on their society. It is not less true that, at the emotional level, the old collective solidarities, by a kind of compensational effect, are becoming once more the place where men secure the roots of their daily life. That these tendencies bring man at the same time towards a universal consciousness and a strong awareness of his own kind is a contradiction in appearance only

— the old contradiction of heart and head, of technique and poetry. French Canadians share these tendencies. Although they are becoming more and more open to the world and less and less disposed to hide behind their "traditional reserve," still they want to survive as a people and to be in charge of their own destiny.

Geography and history have combined to place Quebeckers in an area completely dominated by two peoples of Anglo-Saxon descent: the Americans to the south, and the English Canadians to the west, to the east, and more or less everywhere in the territory of Quebec itself. Now, Quebec is politically dominated by Canada, which is itself an economic and political satellite of the United States. The position of Quebec is far from comfortable. Why not become simply a part of the United States? This temptation has arisen at different periods of their history, but French Canadians, who have been acquiring the habit of resistance since 1760, when New France was surrendered to England, have always had hopes of freeing themselves one day. Today these hopes are stronger than ever. In the great intellectual upheaval that began in the early sixties, the idea of a politically independent Quebec arose; it is central to the Quebec question. The question is: will Quebec continue to belong to the Canadian Confederation or will it become independent? Annexation to the United States is a possibility which, because it has not generally been debated, has a certain number of supporters (perhaps 10 per cent). In the year of the centenary of Canadian confederation, on July 24, 1967, General de Gaulle raised the Quebec question to the international level when he cried from the balcony of Montreal's City Hall, "Long live Free Quebec!" The reaction to this cry in Quebec, in Canada and in the world at large shows clearly that the French head of state had penetrated to the heart of the Quebec problem.

Are we witnessing the beginning of the end of two centuries of domination, or rather the last-ditch heroism of a people soon to be engulfed with the rest of Canada in the vast American empire? Though we don't know the ending to our story, it is perhaps worthwhile to bring some information to bear on this question, which appears today in a number of lights. We know the prediction of the great English historian Arnold Toynbee, but let us repeat it here anyway: "If the future of mankind in a unified world is going to be on the whole a happy one, then I would prophesy that there is a future in the Old World for the Chinese, and in the island of North America for the *Canadiens*. Whatever the future of mankind in North America, I feel pretty confident that these French-speaking Canadians, at any rate, will be there at the end of the story."[2] If with Toynbee we believe that the success of peoples is measured in terms of the challenges they confront, then the survival of the Quebeckers up to now represents a challenge successfully met; the challenge of today is to gain independence and to develop as a North American nation: more and more Quebeckers believe that it too will be met. In a survey conducted in 1964, a great majority of young Quebeckers between 18 and 21 believed that "Quebec will one day be independent."[3]

Boys from Montreal	63.5 %
Girls from Montreal	66.1 %
Boys outside of Montreal	53.0 %
Girls outside of Montreal	59.1 %

The Quebec question also has to do with the fact that a population about eight times smaller than that of France inhabits an area three times greater than that of France (600,000 sq. mi.). Quebec possesses a very diversified hydrographic system and abundant lumber and mineral resources. From this point of view, it is one of the richest countries in the world. Already highly industrialized and urbanized, it has an ever-developing communications network. Thanks to the work done for the international exposition in Montreal in 1967, Quebec's metropolis is one of the most dynamic urban agglomerations in the world; it is the fifth most important city on the North American continent.

Why, in a country so vast, so rich and so advanced from many points of view, do we find so much anxiety and frustration? Why so many violent demonstrations, why terrorism? Essentially, because the majority of Quebec's inhabitants benefit only marginally from this industrial and commercial development, and because their culture is constantly menaced by the groups that dominate their country economically and politically. Their language and culture suffer the fate reserved for subjugated, colonized nations. The Quebec question, in 1969, is a question of becoming aware of this domination and this menace.

Almost everyone who lives here agrees that there are serious problems in Quebec, but there are many conflicting explanations for this state of affairs and many proposals to remedy it. The supporters of the status quo, i.e., the Canadian Confederation, say that Quebec has not quite caught up with the rest of Canada; for them, the problem of Quebec is a problem in regional economic disparity, more or less the normal situation in any federated system, as certain regions develop more rapidly than others. The remedy is equally simple: apply the appropriate economic policies to correct this state of affairs. Most federalists see Quebeckers as the authors of their own misfortune: if, instead of electing so many reactionary governments and investing so much energy in defense of their collective rights, each one of them had striven to succeed in his particular field, Quebeckers would be in much better economic shape today. If, instead of holding fast to outmoded practises and obsolete values, they took an active part in the modern life of North America, they would not have to complain about being oppressed. This view implies the thesis (openly stated, moreover) that in Canada there is one people, one nation, one State composed of several ethnic strains — the English- and French-speaking being the two principal ones — and that the government of Canada will take all necessary measures to ensure the continued existence of such a Canada. This is one of the chief replies made to the Quebec question.

The other reply — given by the great majority of Quebeckers — is that a French-speaking nation exists in Quebec and that it has the right to a great measure of political autonomy; for many Quebeckers, this nation has been dominated continually since 1760. Today, in spite of occasional fits of frustration and impatience, it has become aware of this state of domination and struggles for political independence. This is the reply which explains why there should be a Quebec question.

Like all national questions, Quebec's cannot be understood without a minimum of historical perspective. How else might we explain the fact that a people French in origin, the issue of free men, became what some have called "the white niggers of America"? No other descendants of the great colonial powers of Europe find themselves in the same situation as the French of America. All of them achieved national independence — long ago. We need to explain why a group of New World Frenchmen are still asking, in 1969, the question "To be or not to be?"

We are not concerned here with historical speculation. We are interested, first of all, in certain decisive events, and even more in the way history has been written, how it has been taught and how, above all, it has been woven into the tissue of ideologies, i.e., the successive definitions Quebeckers have held of themselves. It is so true that the way one perceives and sums up reality sometimes has as much importance as reality itself. That is why anyone wishing to understand what the Quebec question means today must know above all what it has meant and what it now means to Quebeckers themselves.

Even a Frenchman, or any other French-speaking person for that matter, does not apparently find it easy to grasp the specific qualities of Quebec culture and to understand the Quebec question. Misunderstanding can easily steal in between observer and observed. Because Quebeckers speak French, one might think that there is no difference between them and French-speaking people in Europe or anywhere else. On the other hand, because Quebeckers live in North America and have adopted the most salient features of American culture, one might as quickly conclude that Quebeckers are purely and simply Americans who still speak French, and that they have nothing in common with other French-speaking peoples. These two errors of appraisal are quite frequently made. We do not underline them to promote the belief that the Quebecker is an ineffable entity forever beyond the grasp of the non-Quebecker. This is an attitude too readily espoused by some Quebeckers. Minority groups are tempted to consider that the foreigner, even the sympathetic foreigner, is utterly incapable of penetrating the secrets of the national character of their group, so complex and unique do they appear to themselves. All we wish to say here is that the observer must not rely too much on first impressions. The Quebecker is no longer a metropolitan Frenchman, but neither has he become a North American — Yankee or Canadian. Over the centuries he has forged a different collective personality. We do not mean that it is rich or attractive, worthy of love or repulsive, but simply that the Quebec personality and culture exist, as there once existed on Quebec soil American Indian cultures with distinctive characteristics of their own.

It is not easy for a Frenchman to admit that a branch of his people have taken on different features in the course of history; that at certain moments they seem so close to him, while at others they appear to act in an incomprehensible manner. This mixture of closeness and distance is also part of the Quebec question. It is often in those traits of the Other which seem closest that one perceives differences. Thus the French language, which we share with other peoples, gives rise to misunderstandings. We sometimes attach different meanings to the same words. When the person we saw as being so close appears different, we can suffer serious disappointment. This may be the principal cause of misunderstandings between Frenchmen and Quebeckers.

Finally, the Quebec question is *not* a number of things. A few years ago, a New York film-maker asked me to help him choose some Quebec locations, preferably outside of Montreal. When I asked him why outside of Montreal, he replied that in the countryside he should have the best chance of getting a live sequence of skirmishes in the guerrilla war waged against the British. No, no, no! Let us not imagine that French-speaking people are engaged in armed combat with the English-speaking; let us not imagine either that on the one side we have a people fighting for its independence and on the other a people refusing to grant it. The few bombs that have exploded were as much intended to convince Quebeckers to involve themselves in a national liberation struggle as to warn the other regions of Canada. As in all the early colonial situations, things are not simple. Some Quebeckers have always agreed to collaborate with the Other. In every historical period, French-speaking persons have acted as intermediaries between the two groups, have been integrated with the majority group, and have chosen to attempt to create a people, if not a nation, with the Other. In the last hundred years, for example, three prime ministers of the Canadian Confederation have had French names and a certain number of French-speaking ancestors. The third of these men, Mr. Pierre-Elliott Trudeau, is today the leader of the Liberal party of Canada. In business circles, many French-speaking people vehemently reject the idea of independence for Quebec. Since 1960, the division has become more marked, on the one hand between generations and on the other between the intelligentsia and the business world. The struggle to destroy the status quo is as much a struggle within Quebec, between different population strata, as one against the Ottawa government, where English-speaking members have for one hundred years been dominant by force of numbers. Thus the Quebec question is not so simple as it might seem. Minority group status creates servile habits which in time become second nature. For many years, the greater part of the population has been isolated and under the thumb of certain small elite groups who themselves possessed only a rather truncated view of reality. It has carried on in its traditional ways without being concerned to know where the real power in society lay. Barely in the last ten years have Quebeckers themselves asked the "Quebec question" with some degree of rigour and completeness. As in all national issues, the evil is not all on one side; the Quebec elites are themselves responsible for many unrealistic attitudes and much class egoism. There remains, however, the brutal fact of our defeat and socioeconomic domination, which no Quebecker has been able to eliminate or prevent. This may be the first real chance for Quebeckers to free themselves since 1760. Will they take it? The stakes in Quebec today are high. On the one side we have a centuries-old hope, on the other power and money. This little book intends to examine the chances of each side in detail, and to help the reader to form an opinion on the future of the "Quiet Revolution." Which will win out — the revolution or the quietude?

Chapter 2
From Frenchmen to Habitants

When Champlain founded Quebec in 1608, nearly four centuries ago, the Quebec problem was born. Everything goes back to that. To know where we have got to and how this French adventure in the New World will evolve in the coming years, we must recall some historical facts. Though discovered by Jacques Cartier in 1534, Canada did not really begin to be inhabited until the arrival of Champlain in 1608. From the beginning of the seventeenth century to 1760, no more than 10,000 settlers arrived, divided about equally between the two centuries. Since the population increased slowly and new arrivals had to integrate themselves into the developing colony, the first period of immigration is of capital importance. Georges Langlois, in his study of the history of Quebec's population, writes:

"The first period of immigration must not be minimized, for its importance, even numerically, is considerable, or rather, fundamental. Settlers in this period (and we have seen that they were mostly from Normandy and Perche) had established their control over all the Quebec part of the St. Lawrence. They were the first to be marked by the soil, the kernel of the new population; they were the first to put down roots in the Canadian land and all later immigrants were grafted onto their stock, receiving an initiation into Canadian life from their hands, and asking for their daughters' hand in marriage."[1]

These are the most distant ancestors of modern Quebeckers. It is of interest to know that they were few in number, that they belonged to a relatively homogeneous social stratum, and that they came from those regions of France which were recognizably like those of New France.

"They had served," writes Léon Gérin, "in their homeland something of an early apprenticeship to the

rough life of pioneers and woodsmen they were to encounter in the Laurentian wilds. They had not, in fact,
come from the areas of France where the living was easy,
but rather from the regions of forest, brush, and swamp
which, even at the beginning of the eighteenth century,
occupied large areas of France."[2] The transition does not
appear to have been too abrupt. Not only did the first
settlers come from fairly similar regions — Normandy,
Perche, Poitou, Aunis, Angoumois — but several emigrated
in groups of families and continued their traditional life on
arrival here. While looking forward to making a living from
the soil eventually, the settlers rapidly became involved in
the fur trade.

New France for the most part escaped the effects of
the disintegration crises common to frontier countries. The
immigrants were relatively speaking very homogeneous;
the men of the Church had a considerable influence on the
budding colony; the Indians were a menace obliging the
settlers to unite among themselves. These circumstances
appear to have given rise early to a society which acquires
a structure because internal factors — values, institutions,
language and religion — contribute to its unity and, on the
other hand, the external environment — war against the
Iroquois and the harshness of physical conditions — forces
the Quebeckers to unite in order to survive. Soon other
factors will appear which will make them yet more homogeneous. The *"habitants"* — those who inhabit New France
permanently, roughly those who till the soil, who have
decided to establish themselves here — will come to look
upon themselves as different from the transients, the
Frenchmen, the administrators — from those who are not
settled in New France for good. The *habitants*, the permanent settlers, are mostly rural; the French, the metro-
politans, live in the towns. A lesser tradition begins to
develop, i.e., a culture adapted to the country and above
all oral, which over the years distinguishes itself from the
"great tradition," the written tradition. "The great tradition is cultivated in schools or temples; the little tradition

works itself out and keeps itself going in the lives of the unlettered in their village communities. The tradition of the philosopher, theologian, and literary man is a tradition consciously cultivated and handed down; that of the little people is for the most part taken for granted and not submitted to much scrutiny or considered refinement and improvement."[3] This little tradition appears under the French regime, before 1760, and becomes very important after the Conquest. The greater part of the population will live by it for many years.

To explain what will become of this Quebec people left to its own devices after the Conquest, it is important to note that, even under the French regime, this people has already become more homogeneous than the French who lived in about the same conditions in the French provinces. What was New France before 1760? "By 1700," according to Jacques Henripin, "natural increase and immigration, the largest waves of which arrived between 1663 and 1671, had raised the population to about 15,000."[4] These 15,000 persons formed a group of French settlers whose social and cultural institutions were beginning to differ from those of the metropolis, from which they were much more cut off than the rural communities of France of the same era. "In 1721," to quote Henripin again, "this riparian population (established on the banks of the St. Lawrence) was divided into 82 parishes, 48 on the left bank and 34 on the right. At that time three agglomerations had an urban character: Quebec, Montreal, and Three-Rivers."[5]

Already, under the French regime, conditions are established which will make this people of New France begin to distinguish itself from the metropolis; they draw in on themselves to create, here on American soil, another French-speaking people. French institutions are modified, habits change, and another mentality is born.

A new kind of human being will appear: the French-Canadian *habitant*. This man lives within an institution as unique as himself: the row settlement.

Sociologists have perhaps not insisted enough on the uniqueness of the *habitant* as a social type. Geographers, however, have not failed to underline the originality of the row settlement form of community. For Max Derruau, the row settlement is "the establishment of houses in a single file — along a riverbank or road — a short distance away from one another, each at the end of its parcel of land. A man's property extends back at right angles to the direction of the river's flow, forming a long narrow strip parallel to the neighbouring farm. Each tenant has frontage on the river and, later, on the highway. He can seek help from his nearest neighbour, and the section of road he must maintain (and keep free of snow) is as small as possible for the acreage of the farm, which stretches back perpendicular to the road."[6] This unique form of settlement is the work of the Quebec *habitant* (and let us insist once again on his originality as a social type). What influences shaped this *habitant*, gradually cut off from the great tradition and isolated from other social strata, yet destined to become the pivot of a Quebec society?

The Quebec sociologist Jean-Charles Falardeau has compared the parish of New France to that which existed in France during the same period, the seventeenth century. In France, social and political power was split among three main institutions: the village assembly, the lord of the manor, and the parish priest. Here are Falardeau's comments on the village assembly:

"The assemblies of villagers deliberated issues and saw that their measures were carried out. Everywhere in France they constituted the core of village life from medieval times on. Everybody, or almost everybody, belonged, and everything concerning the life of the community was there discussed, decided, and voted upon ... Somehow protected by its very weakness, but jealously aware of its growing solidarity and responsibility, the village community was precociously democratic; the assembly gave it an organic unity, familial in character."[7] Of the role of the manor lord Falardeau says: "Although the village, in the seventeenth century, owns property and partially governs itself with a view to its own interests, it largely continues to depend on the man who formerly ruled it by royal right. The lord of the manor is still the community's immediate superior . . . like the church, the castle dominates the village; the lord readily assumes the role of protector for his vassals. His authority is sometimes cordial: he settles differences, intervenes in trials, and pays a visit to the thatched cottages . . . The manor lord is, in sum, an antiquated but respected figure. The village continues to define itself for the most part in relation to the manor."[8] The parish priest is found in both the French and the Canadian parishes: his role in France is as follows: "Mainspring of community life, the parish priest himself submits to all kinds of local restrictions; the churchwardens limit his authority in the secular administration of the parish, and his influence over communal life is mitigated by the rights of the villagers. He attends community meetings but is not by rights a magistrate or councillor; by decree of the provincial governors, he acquires a right to these posts at the end of the seventeenth century. Because of his education he is made the municipal secretary, but only to serve the interests of the community. In the words of Viscount d'Avenel, the parish priest 'is something of a mayor, but the mayor is even more something of a parish priest.'"[9]

Falardeau adds: "Readily disregarding the priest's wishes, the parishioners often not only determine the hours for mass, organize the service and appoint the cantors or other church employees (whom the priest cannot divest of their office without the consent of the parishioners), but also select the preachers they want for Advent or Lent. In this regard the church was almost a communal institution."[10]

Such then are the three characteristic institutions of the French rural parish in the seventeenth century: village assembly, manor lord, parish priest. Falardeau adds that the church had almost become an institution run by the community. What do we find in the French-Canadian parish in the seventeenth century? The New World colony, cut off from the mainstream of national life, had to transform the institutions and traditions of the mother country in its new environment. Thus the manor economy in Quebec was from the beginning very different from what it was in France. Feudalism in France was essentially a political institution whose roots reached several centuries into the past; in New France, its function was chiefly economic. The manor lords were looked upon as land-office agents; their job was to parcel out the territory and see it brought under cultivation. The manor lord in seventeenth-century France was still, in his parish, a force to be reckoned with; in Quebec, his role shrunk in importance. The *habitants* of New France spontaneously adopted a pattern of settlement which made it impossible for the administrators of the colony to group them in villages, as the king had ordered. Strung out along the river, their dwellings were not gathered around a central core as in French villages; the row settlement, rather than the village, was the basic social unit in Canada. Far from constantly playing the part of "the big farm boss," as Gérin[11] calls him, the manor lord soon becomes interested in administration and war, leaving the settlers to live by themselves on their land. This change has two results: the peasant quickly grows accustomed to more independence and liberty than he enjoyed in France; secondly, he soon becomes used to life in a small, close group where each individual is roughly the equal of any other, and all share the same ideal of life. As Falardeau says: "The French-Canadian *habitant* is personally devoted to his land, which he cultivates freely with the help of his family. His neighbours are other *habitants* engaged in the same work, and this community of interests, fostered by the close proximity of the houses stretching along the same road, creates a spirit of mutual aid of a type unknown in the French countryside. Neighbours help each other out, visit back and forth. The new shore settlement will become in

Canada the basic unit of social solidarity."[12] This type of settlement differed from the usual nuclear village of France, and the manor lord in Quebec did not represent, as in France, a social element markedly distinct from the community.

The political and social institution of the manor lord, as we find it in French villages, was missing in Quebec. Into this power vacuum there walked the parish priest, destined to play a great part in all Quebec's history. The religious institution of the parish was to outstrip all others, political or social. In France, three institutions tended to achieve equilibrium among themselves, or at least, each one carried a certain weight and expressed a certain bias. In Quebec, the parish priest stood alone. There was no manor lord, no municipal council, and above all no village assembly. Gustave Lanctôt, a specialist in the administration of New France, writes: "The inhabitants of New France had no conception of collective action on the political level. Lacking any organization to group and direct them, they acquired the habit of submitting passively to orders issued by the colonial administrators, the governor and the king."[13] The Quebec *habitant* soon grows used to a passive existence socially and politically; his life becomes more homogeneous, more submerged in the group, and more imbued with religion. These tendencies grow stronger in time, as Falardeau points out in the following passage: "Social intercourse among neighbours was to be, for the French-Canadian *habitants*, almost the only form of activity outside the family. They attached no importance, if not no meaning, to life in a secular municipality. We need hardly recall that there was never, throughout the entire period of French rule in Canada, any organization of the territory into incorporated towns. As the religious organisms, the parishes, were gradually established, they provided an adequate administrative framework in themselves, fulfilling the function of rural municipalities."[14] The parish and the clergy were to make Quebec society take on a uniform religious character. Every problem of village life, education for example, will find a solution in organizations corollary to the Church, especially the church councils. "Properly municipal concerns were to remain strictly in the parish domain."[15] The parish priest soon becomes more than the undisputed head of the parish; he plays a part in every aspect of community life. "Not a single transaction took place in the parish without consulting the priest. He drew up wills, drafted deeds of gift, and looked after documents placed in his care."[16] The parish priest was to become, in the words of Gérin, "the most powerful bond of parish life . . . the natural protector and representative of the *habitant*."[17] From the time of French rule education was in the hands of the clergy; through the church council, which he usually controlled, the priest became the keystone of the educational system. "The church council of the parish, when the opportunity presented itself, took the initiative and responsibility of founding the few rural primary schools that existed under French rule. There were eighty such schools at the end of the seventeenth century, open to all without tuition. Almost all of them were run by religious congregations, especially by the women of these congregations, or else by some teacher or the priest himself."[18] As Falardeau so rightly observes, the parish succeeds, after some years, "in realizing the clergy's ideal social program, essentially an intimate community of families." What part does the *habitant* play in this parish where he will spend most of his life? Léon Gérin remarks: "The *habitant* did not establish the institution of the parish: he found it ready-made, entered into it, received its stamp. He does not dominate the parish, he is dominated by it."[19] "At no time," says Falardeau, "did the French-Canadian *habitant* play an active part in the life or government of his parish community; nor was he capable of so doing."[20]

This examination of the parish in seventeenth-century Quebec and France seems to lead us to a first conclusion. By a reduction of the elements that compose and direct it, the parish structure in Canada becomes simplified and homogeneous. As this transformation was due to the actions of the Quebec clergy, we ought now to ask ourselves what manner of religion was practised by this clergy and their faithful flocks. In other words, did the religion taught and practised in Canada favour the great tradition or rather tend to isolate Quebeckers even more?

Let us first note that in France, with Bossuet, Catholicism takes on a strong flavour of gallicanism, while in Quebec Monseigneur de Laval and the Jesuits successfully combat this trend and establish, on the contrary, a tradition of ultramontanism that has lasted to our own day. To understand the type of society which developed under French rule, we must realize that the influence of the Church, and from 1635 onwards that of the Jesuits especially, was much more constant and decisive than the influence of the political metropolis. Parkman, the American historian of Canada, wrote of the Church: "More even than the royal power, she shaped the character and the destinies of the colony . . . The royal government was transient; the Church was permanent. The English conquest shattered the whole apparatus of civil administration at a blow, but it left her untouched."[21]

Mgr. de Laval, who dominated religious life in Canada from 1659 to 1684, has had the greatest influence on the formation of this Quebec ethos. After much discussion and haggling with Rome and the French government, he managed to have the bishop of Quebec directly appointed by, and subordinate to, the Holy See. As Mason Wade, author of a history of French Canadians, says: ". . . ultramontanism triumphed in New France under the championship of Bishop Laval, who vanquished the gallicanism of governor and intendant and established for himself a position which the Pope himself might have envied. Ever since, French Canada has remained a stronghold of clericalism. . . ."[22]

The tendency of the French-Canadian clergy to subordinate State to Church dates from Laval. In his violent disputes with the civil administrators he offered an example to his successors, who also wanted a say in the governing of the State. The Church took exclusive control of parishes, aligned itself with Rome rather than France, and in theory and practise supported the non-separation of Church and State. It thereby favoured the evolution of a truly homogeneous people.

In 1664 Pierre Boucher published a *True and Natural History of the Customs and Products of the Land of New France, Commonly Called Canada.* In presenting Boucher, the modern historian Wade says that his remarks illustrate the theocentric nature of the colony and the growing distinction between transient Frenchmen and those who had cast their lot with the colony. Pierre Boucher writes: "In a word, people may live a very happy life here if they are virtuous, but not if they are lacking in this respect, for they are under too close a surveillance; thus I do not recommend to the unvirtuous that they come here, for they would be run out of the colony or at least forced to leave, as has happened to many. These persons are precisely the country's harshest critics, because they have failed to find what they were looking for."[23]

The baron of Lahontan also perceives the differences existing between Canada and France. He complains bitterly of the priests: "You can hardly enjoy a game of cards or pay a call on a lady without coming to the attention of some priest who is sure to denounce you from his pulpit on high. In his zeal he goes so far as to name the offending parties; if I tell you that he will go so far as to refuse communion to noble ladies who wear coloured ribbons, you can figure out the rest for yourself. You can scarcely imagine the extent of the authority accruing to these princes of the Church. As far as I am concerned their behaviour is ridiculous. They excommunicate people who wear masks, even going after them wherever they are to unmask them and heap disgrace upon them; they watch over the conduct of daughters and wives more than fathers and husbands could. They persecute those who do not take communion every month and, at Easter, they force everybody to reveal them their personal histories in the confessional. They forbid and burn all books which are not devotional. I cannot think of this tyranny without a cry of protest against the tactless zeal of the priest of this town. This cruel person entered the house of my host one day, and seeing some books on my table, he hurled himself upon my Petronius, a book I cherish as the apple of my eye, for it's an unexpurgated version. He tore up all its pages in such a fury that had my host not held me back when I saw the remains, I would have pounced on him and torn out the hairs of his beard as he had torn out the pages of my book. They are not content to examine the deeds of men; they want to pry into their very thoughts. Judge by this, sir, of the pleasures we enjoy here."²⁴ Lahontan also complains that the French Canadians set little store by their cousins, the Frenchmen.

Montreal soon became the focus of commerce in the colony while Quebec remained the administrative centre. One of the most important sociological traits of this population is that two social classes develop fully under French rule: the elite, consisting of administrators, higher clergy, and those who have recently been referred to as middle-class gentlemen; then suddenly, almost without intermediaries, the mass of *habitants* living in parishes, the row settlements with their parish priest.

This division of the population corresponds to two further distinctions. The elite tended to be above all French, recently arrived in the country; the mass of *habitants* were French-Canadian. Secondly, the elite lived in urban agglomerations, the *habitants* in small rural communities. We shall see that, after the Conquest, these three elements will have a powerful effect in shaping Quebec's future.

The French-Canadian ethnic group, mostly *habitants* living outside the cities, rather quickly develops its own peculiarities, growing away from the French type of society and life style. Father Charlevoix describes French-

Canadian life in these terms: "Everyone has the where-withal of existence here; one pays little to the King; the *habitant* knows not the *taille*; he has cheap bread; meat and fish are not dear; but wine, cloth, and all things that must come from France cost a great deal. The gentlemen and officers, who have only their pay and who are charged with families, are the worst off. The women usually bring no other dowry to their husbands than much wit, love, their charms, and a great fertility; for God bestows upon the marriages in this country the benediction that he gave to those of the patriarchs; to provide subsistence for such numerous families requires that one also lead the life of the patriarchs ... We know no healthier climate in the world than there; there is no special sickness, the country-side and forest are full of marvellous remedies, and the trees distill balms of great virtue. These advantages should at least retain those whom Providence has caused to be born there, but frivolity, aversion to assiduous and regular labor, and the spirit of independence have always made a number of young men leave, and have prevented the colony from peopling itself."[25]

Father Charlevoix then mentions an imponderable factor which must have played an important part in the transformation of Frenchmen into Quebeckers: the Indian influence on the budding society. The Indian influence has left few traces where intellectual culture is concerned, but has left more of a mark on the life style of the people themselves. The Indians of the New World were perfectly adapted to the country. They couldn't help but influence the French-Canadian settlers, giving them something of their own taste for the wide-open spaces and the free life. Most chroniclers report that the Quebeckers and the Indians of eastern Canada have always got along well together. The general attitude that the Quebeckers adopted towards the Indians, so different from that of the English, shows that they had a certain sympathy for one another. We must remember that marriage between Indians and whites has always been more common among the

French Canadians than among the English. Father Charlevoix, enumerating the faults of the French Canadians, says
that these are also the faults of the Red Men. "It seems,"
he says, "that the air which one breathes in this continent
contributes to [them], but the example and the habits of
its natural inhabitants, who put all their happiness in
liberty and independence, are more than sufficient to form
this character."[26] The Jesuit notes that the French
Canadians like to dress well even if they have to sacrifice
some of the pleasures of the table. He compares the
Quebec colonist to his English neighbour: "The English
colonist amasses means and makes no superfluous expense;
the French enjoys what he has and often parades what he
has not. The former works for his heirs; the latter leaves
his in the need in which he is himself, to get along as best
they can. The British Americans dislike war, because they
have so much to lose; they do not humour the Savages,
because they see no need to do so. The French youth, on
the contrary, loathe peace and get along well with the
natives, whose esteem they easily win in war and whose
friendship they always earn."[27]

One can only conclude that under French rule the
French settlers were on the way to becoming Quebeckers,
that the type of society they were forming had evolved to
the point where even the priests could no longer get along
with their French colleagues. In 1730, Mgr. Dosquet will
complain of the audacious and independent spirit of
Canadian priests. They have become so insolent, he adds,
"that three of them are enough to become the masters of
the country and overthrow the bishops . . . The canons do
not care to recognize laws, statutes, or even superiors.
They treat their dean as an inferior and their bishop as an
equal."[28]

At the end of French rule, when New France is ceded
to England in 1760, a new nation is plainly taking root in
American soil. The French have become Quebec *habitants*
little by little; they begin to reveal certain character and
behaviour traits which differentiate them more and more

from metropolitan Frenchmen. Bougainville, who comes to Quebec in 1756 as aide to Montcalm, remarks that the French Canadians are "vainglorious, mendacious, obliging, kindly, honest; tireless for hunting, racing, and journeys to the *pays d'en haut*; lazy at cultivation of the land." He notes that "a very great deal of brandy was drunk here" and that "there was little concern for the education of youth, since one early devoted oneself to hunting and warfare . . . It must be granted that despite this lack of education the Canadians have natural wit, speak with ease, although they do not know how to write; their accent is as good as Paris; their diction is full of vicious phrases borrowed from the Indian tongues or of nautical terms used in ordinary style." Bougainville refers to the increasing differences between Frenchmen and Quebeckers: "It seems," he writes, "that we are of a different nation, even an enemy one."[29]

When Quebeckers are thus left to themselves in the St. Lawrence valley, they already form a distinct group of French people. Let us note that in New France the social classes are less sharply defined than in France. The manor lord of New France is an entrepreneur whose job is to settle *habitants* on land granted him by the State; he remains close to them. Because many manors are given to *habitants*, they become lords themselves. The *habitant* acquires a certain social mobility which makes him a social type quite different from the French peasant. The lord is something of a *habitant*, but the *habitant* is himself something of a lord. Let us quote this passage drawn from the first Canadian novel, *The History of Emily Montague*, by Frances Brooke: ". . . you scarce see the meanest peasant walking; even on horseback appears to them a fatigue insupportable; you see them lolling at ease, like their lazy lords, in carrioles and calashes, according to the season; a boy to guide the horse on a seat in front of the carriage, too lazy even to take the trouble of driving themselves . . . ."[30] The novelist adds, in speaking of the *habitants*: "They are excessively vain, and not only look on the French as the only civilized nation in the world, but on themselves as the flower of the French nation: they had, I am told, a great aversion to the regular troops which came from France in the late war . . . ."[31] The baroness de Riedesel observes the manners of the *habitants* shortly after the Conquest: "The country I have passed through is very picturesque. Each *habitant* has a fine house which he carefully whitewashes every year. The sons of the family, and the sons-in-law who marry into it, build themselves very pretty parishes close to the parents, who see the family grow rapidly around them. For this reason these people call themselves *habitants* (dwellers) rather than peasants."

These *habitants* are the people who will continue the Quebec nation after the Conquest.

Chapter 3
The Defeated Keep the Faith

The *habitants* and the priests remain alone (or almost alone) with the English in Voltaire's acres of snow,[1] grappling with the long winters, poverty and the problems of survival. The long hibernation of Quebec which is beginning will know periods of storm and of calm, but will be above all characterized by small victories gained at great cost, and forever threatened anew. Never did the spring breakup take so long to come: two hundred years.

The surrender of New France to England had two immediate results: the ruling class of the country was decapitated, and the French Canadians were forced to concentrate themselves even more in the rural parishes. The two coming together created a premature abolition of social classes. The process had begun in the period before the Conquest, when the *habitants* had become much freer and more independent than the French peasants and when many lords of the manor had become to some degree *habitants* themselves; it now became more accentuated. There is nothing tragic about the equalization, on the contrary. The tragedy is that all Quebec becomes a subjugated ethnic class. The difficulties between the social classes or the estates tend to diminish in French-Canadian society itself, but the gulf between the two societies of those who rule and those who are ruled has a tendency to widen. From the Conquest on, the English administration will ally itself with the Quebec clergy and with what remains of the aristocracy. This is the "aristocratic compact" referred to by historians. Alfred Dubuc says of it: "The strategy of creating an aristocratic society on the banks of the St. Lawrence, to dominate the popular forces and check the republican aspirations of the rising middle class, relied upon the participation of three social groups interested in maintaining the structure of the Old Order:

the British Army officers and high colonial administrators, the French-Canadian manor lords and, finally, the Catholic Church. The aristocratic compact worked smoothly as long as new forces did not threaten the social order."[2] We shall see that the *habitants* are left more and more to themselves in the countryside, with their parish priest and their oral traditions.

How did the Quebeckers react to the defeat and to their change of allegiance? A contemporary historian, Michel Brunet, says this: "All the historians have emphasized the very cordial relations which were established between the French Canadians and their conquerors from the first months of the English occupation. The fact is undeniable ... Should we be surprised that the majority accepted their fate without protest? It even appears that several French Canadians whom we may judge guilty of mindlessness were delighted by the change of rulers. Fearing the worst, the vanquished discovered to their astonishment that the conqueror treated them with benevolence. Their exaggerated fear explains, in good part, their almost spontaneous submission at the beginning of the English occupation."[3] One might also invoke the profound divisions afflicting the country at the end of the French era. Some historians have even maintained that without the internal clashes, especially between Montcalm and Vaudreuil, the outcome of the war might have been different. One should also mention the extortions and scandals of which Bigot and his clique were guilty to understand that the French Canadians had become very unsympathetic towards the French administration, which reflected upon their attitude towards France and its representatives. The reactions of victors and vanquished alike might be partially explained by the fact that ideological warfare as we know it in the twentieth century scarcely existed in the eighteenth. Wars did not yet have the total, global character they were to acquire later on; men conquered not to convert a people or change their ideology, but to acquire political power and economic profit from a colony or a country. The English and French who faced each other in Canada were the representatives or the descendants of the two greatest nations of Europe, nations which respected one another. Religion was the most serious barrier between these two groups: one was papist, the other antipapist. This factor was to play a very important part in the growing differentiation between the two groups.

It seems that the higher clergy — as so often later on — set the tone in rallying to England. From 1775 on, Mgr. Briand writes: "They say of me, as of you, that I am English . . . I am English, in fact; you ought to be; they [the French Canadians] ought to be too, because they have given their word, and all the natural, divine, and human laws command them to be so. But neither I, nor you, nor they need be of the English religion. That is what these poor folk do not understand; they are under English sway only in their political life . . . ."[4] After the Conquest, the French-Canadian clergy, thanks to its benevolent attitude towards the English, was to acquire a more solid position than the one it had enjoyed under French rule. From this era dates the predominant influence that the Church was to maintain throughout Quebec history.

The French-Canadian colony had in 1760 a certain secular elite comprising soldiers, administrators and businessmen. This secular elite was usually recruited among the French, and lived above all in the cities. What happened to these social classes after the Conquest? Some historians have offered what is a somewhat oversimplified reply: the French departed, the French Canadians stayed behind. Yet it does seem that, if things did not happen exactly that way, the result was almost the same as though all the French had left en masse. Michel Brunet, in considering the problems of how the English Conquest influenced the French-Canadian middle class, writes: "Seeking an explanation for the absence of an elite, particularly in the cultural field — a state of affairs he was acutely ashamed of — Michel Bibaud attributed this fact to the emigration of the ruling class after the Conquest. He asserted that between one thousand and twelve hundred French or French Canadians had left the colony." He concludes: "This reduction in the French-Canadian population was all the more regrettable because it occurred in the upper class, the only group, with few exceptions, that had developed its talents and acquired some degree of knowledge. This change for the worse, in the field of the arts and sciences, was felt for a long time in the country."[5] Brunet adds: "Finally, in 1899, Judge Louis-François Georges Baby published a detailed study in which he proved, with figures to back him up, that there had not been a massive emigration of the ruling classes. Even if it was not massive, however, emigration considerably reduced the number of ruling families."[6] Robert de Roquebrune estimates that two thousand people left Canada for France after the Conquest. Those who went away seem to have come especially from the ruling class: administrators, nobles, new arrivals in Canada.

Historians may agree that members of the ruling class did not emigrate in large numbers, but few have asked what happened to those who remained in Canada. Who were they? Brunet is aware of the part played by the bourgeoisie[7] in the development of the European countries, the United States and English Canada. The Quebec bourgeoisie, for him, consists of those members of the ruling class who stayed in Canada and tried to survive under the English regime. Though this was certainly a very small bourgeoisie compared to those of other countries or even to the class which had begun to develop in Quebec at the end of the French regime, its destiny under English rule is significant. "We must remember," says Brunet, "that the businessmen who remained in the country were the poorest and neediest ones . . . They did not belong to the group of big businessmen, monopolists and war profiteers. The great majority of them formed the lower level of the French-Canadian capitalist bourgeoisie, the level of small entrepreneurs with modest resources and no great influence. Their limited finances and mediocre personal ability had kept them from the first ranks of the business world. Moreover, they had not enjoyed official protection, as they did not belong to the privileged clique. They were the most vociferous spokesmen of the nameless crowd of malcontents, and they were the severest critics of the Bigot administration and of the scandalous successes of their more fortunate rivals, who had been associated with the provincial administrator or protected by him."[7] The historian seems to imply that the richest and most important part of the bourgeoisie had already left, for he deals only with what he himself calls the second level of the middle class. All these people were not entirely displeased at the departure of the French. "The citizens of Montreal — priests, nobles and middle class — from the month of February 1762 were in no way backward about recalling the abuses of the French colonial administration. According to them, it had reduced the 'merchants of the country' to the role of 'tranquil spectators of a commerce that ought to have belonged to them' ("Petition of the citizens of Montreal to His Majesty the King of England," February 12, 1762, in *Documents relatifs à la monnaie, au change, et aux finances du Canada sous le régime français,* Ottawa, 1925, 2, 970)." The bourgeoisie of Quebec had docilely accepted the decrees of the Supreme Being which had made them 'subjects of our new monarch.' They had no doubt that the latter would heap his favours and goodwill upon them. As vanquished subjects, had they not been deeply impressed by the sweetness, justice and moderation of his government? (Address given by the citizens of Quebec on the establishment of the peace treaty, June 4, 1763, in Auguste Gosselin's *L'Eglise du Canada après la conquête,* Quebec, 1916-1917, 1, pp. 59-60.) Brunet later shows how what was left of this bourgeoisie was ruined. "A series of misfortunes befell them. The bankruptcy of the French government partially ruined French-Canadian businessmen. Almost all their liquid capital was in the form of paper money and letters of exchange drawn on the public treasury. They only recovered a small part of it; we do not know exactly how much they lost in this unhappy venture. The Conquest had reoriented the economic life of the colony, and not in favour of the new subjects of His Britannic Majesty. The French-Canadian merchants found themselves completely helpless; partially ruined by the bankruptcy of the French treasury, they were unable to take delivery of the goods they had ordered before the end of the war, which deprived them of their old sources of supply. Their situation had something tragic about it." Forced out of the export trade, they were soon dislodged from the fur trade which had so flourished during the French period. In Brunet's words, "The fur trade required serious investment of capital. The canoes sent into the interior had to be provisioned and the crews paid. All but totally deprived of credit, the French-Canadian merchants saw themselves slowly evicted from the fur trade." Brunet illustrates the degree to which French Canadians had lost out in commerce: 'The Quebec City directory, published in 1790, has some revealing information. The capital had thirty-seven merchants or dealers, of which only four were French-Canadian or French' (Hugh MacKay, *The Directory of the City and Suburbs of Quebec,* Quebec, 1790).[8] Brunet's demonstration is well researched and convincing. Those merchants, businessmen and dealers who stayed behind were unable to survive the Conquest; they were obliged to limit themselves to small retail operations. This was to be their lot for many years to come.

The businessmen were eliminated. What became of the nobles? The greatest cordiality was soon established between the manor lords and the English officers; the many marriages contracted by officers in the colony attest the intimacy of their relations. Wade adds: "Murray and Burton exchanged letters to settle the problems of 'matrimonial fever,' and the wife of the Quebec garrison's chaplain noted that the French-Canadian women had a 'great penchant for the English officers.'"[9] Brunet writes of the colonial nobility: "Its fate was no happier than that of the French-Canadian businessmen. The greater part of the nobility was not rich. The few well-to-do families had grown wealthy in commerce. Their future was that of other French Canadians engaged in trade."[10] Brunet continues: "The military defeat of the country had discredited the old ruling class in the eyes of the masses (see Daniel, De Lery 72). Its servility towards the conquerors removed from it the little prestige it retained. This is why it proved incapable of rallying the peasants at the time of the American invasion. This humiliating defeat diminished its usefulness in the eyes of the conqueror. Without a fortune and with large families to support, it sunk into mediocrity. Some of its members nevertheless had the illusion that they had a political part to play up to the end of the eighteenth century. After 1800, a new generation made itself the spokesman of the French-Canadian population. As for the nobility, it continued to disappear either by assimilation, begun from the first months of the English occupation, or by the exile of its children, obliged to flee an occupied homeland where the old ruling classes had had to yield their place to the conquerors."[11]

We have called these historians to witness for the fact that after the Conquest Quebec society, far from continuing to develop like other Western societies of the era, becoming industrial, urbanized and secular, on the contrary draws inwards upon its popular and rural elements and, instead of become more urbanized, becomes more folklike. We observe, among other phenomena, a greater predominance of agricultural occupations; a greater scattering of the population among the rural parishes; more social homogeneity; reinforcement of moral and religious norms; less important internal stratification and differentiation; and, finally, a more restricted territorial, occupational, and upward mobility.

After the Conquest Quebec becomes more isolated and more homogeneous than it had ever been before.

Englishmen are present in greater and greater numbers, which makes the French-speaking people aware that they form a distinct group. Contacts with France and Frenchmen become rarer and rarer. August Viatte, the historian of French literature in America, remarks that "The St. Lawrence valley is treated as a private preserve. Even though he is an emigrant, a great noble like the Duke of La Rochefoucauld-Liancourt cannot obtain, in 1795, the authorization to visit it . . . "[12]

Quebeckers cut themselves off, withdrawing ever further into their rural communities. Pushed out of commerce and administration, they have nothing to do but cultivate the soil. Later on, historians will say that they withdrew to avoid assimilation, but it seems that this retreat was due more to economic than to ideological imperatives. "People begin to talk of a return to the land," says Michel Brunet. "Agriculture is a refuge for the French Canadians who have been eliminated from their country's commercial life. Many former tax farmers and merchants turn to agriculture from necessity."[13]

Statistics give us some idea of the extent of the ruralization in Canada during the first sixty-five years of English control. At the end of the French period the population was three-quarters rural, i.e., about one quarter of the people lived in the cities. The kind of city we are dealing with at this time is clearly not comparable to the city we find with the development of industrial civilization. Still, we can say that one quarter of the population around 1760 is not involved in agriculture and lives in an urban environment. Thirty years later, in 1790, the rural population has increased to 80 per cent; in another thirty-five years, by 1825, the rural inhabitants constitute 88 per cent of the population.[14] It is hard to verify these figures, but the information seems to refer only to French-speaking people. The population retains this strongly rural character for fifty years; in 1871, it was still only 19.9 per cent urban. It is only after the First World War that Quebec begins to be noticeably urbanized; today the urban population of Quebec is 80 per cent of the total.

Another demographic factor initiates a trend opposite to that we generally associate with urbanization: the increasing fertility of French-Canadian women after the Conquest. The demographer Jacques Henripin tells us: "During the French Regime, except for some exceptional periods, the rate of increase of the Canadian population does not support Malthus' hypothesis that, if unrestricted, population will double every twenty-five years ... Surprisingly enough, during the English domination, from 1760 to 1850, French-Canadian population did effectively double every twenty-five years, and probably without any substantial *net* immigration." The demographer then asks if this fertility is exceptional: "It seems that Canadian marital fertility during the eighteenth century (and the first half of the nineteenth century as well), was exceptionally high." To give an idea of the increase in the French-Canadian population, Henripin adds: "During the last two centuries, world population has multiplied by three, European population by four, and French-Canadian population by eighty, in spite of net emigration which can be estimated roughly at 800,000."[15]

Here is an exceptional phenomenon. Almost an entire people is forced, in order to survive, to concentrate itself on its peasantry, on its *habitants*. For the French historian Henri Marrou, Quebec after the Conquest goes far back into history: "We should not look upon it as a survival of the Old Regime, or even of the Middle Ages. As in our own Merovingian period, the French-Canadian clergy found itself, in 1763, the only representative of the national conscience and the national culture, the only elite. The French character would not have endured so triumphantly if, in 1763, the Catholic Church had only reached the missionary stage; fortunately, however, it was already solidly organized, with a bishop, parish priests, a whole clergy and — a most important thing — a seminary to educate it."[16]

One of the immediate effects of the regression

referred to by Marrou is the massive increase in illiteracy. According to Viatte, "In 1827, of 87,000 signatures on a petition to Governor Dalhousie, 78,000 names are indicated only with a cross . . . Since the Conquest there have been two generations of illiterates."[17] Edmond Roy, in going over the history of the Lauzon manor farm, writes: "In their isolation in the depths of their farms; in the continuity of their manual labour; perhaps also because of the paucity of their resources, the *habitants* of Lauzon remained almost completely ignorant of any intellectual luxury, any idea of art, science, or literature . . . barely 10 per cent had learned, imperfectly, to read and write in childhood, to do an addition, perhaps to sing in the church. Once out of school, good-bye to reading and writing!"[18] The manor he speaks of here, Lauzon, is situated in the centre of Quebec province, near the city of Quebec; it is no disfavoured, peripheral region.

The French Revolution occurs shortly after the Conquest. From the ideological point of view, it serves to isolate Quebec culture from French culture and from the rest of Occidental civilization. Two concepts of France develop; the good France, pre-1789, and the bad, postrevolutionary France. After the Conquest, Quebec is organized as a traditional society, a folk society, but it still retains some ties with the great tradition of France. Her overall culture, then, is based on oral tradition, but some connections are maintained with the rest of the Western world, thanks primarily to the clergy. The Church and the clergy, while they give to this society a strongly religious orientation, also prevent it from becoming tribal. Religion will be the unifier for this society, the common denominator of all the small rural communities where the majority of Quebec's population will be concentrated. Though the clergy itself loses touch somewhat with the great tradition, yet it preserves reading and writing and adheres quite closely to the Catholicism of Rome.

Shortly after the Conquest, the French Canadians obtain guarantees that they will be able to go on practising their religion, speaking their language and using the French civil code. In 1791 England grants representative government to Canada, dividing the country into Upper and Lower Canada (Lower Canada is more or less equivalent to contemporary Quebec). Representative government was the direct result of the American and French revolutions rather than an effect of English goodwill towards Canada. We should not see it as the result of struggles undertaken by Quebeckers; in general, they were rather opposed to this form of government. The English merchants who had invaded French Canada after the Conquest were the ones who fought hardest for representative government. Dorchester, the governor of Canada, candidly admits it in an archive document cited by Wade: "Dorchester's reply . . . pointed out that as assembly was demanded chiefly by the English merchants of Quebec and Montreal, while *habitants* were neutral in the matter and the *seigneurs* opposed . . ."[19] Some historians claim that the American and French revolutions gave French Canadians a taste for parliamentary representation; if so, this enthusiasm disappeared after the first election which followed the Constitutional Act of 1791. The French Canadians, about fourteen-fifteenths of Lower Canada's population, obtained only three-quarters of the seats in the legislative assembly; moreover, the French Canadians were a minority in the Legislative Council (seven out of sixteen) and in the Executive Council (four out of nine). In administrative posts their minority was even more marked. They straightway learned to distrust democracy and representative government. Lord Durham remarked a few years later that the French Canadians were not ready for representative government; how could they adjust to influencing the destiny of the State when they had not even had anything to do with running their own parishes?

According to Durham, the jump was too great. How could it be otherwise? Cut off from its elite, withdrawn into itself in rural communities, practising a subsistence economy, French-Canadian folk society had trouble get-

ting interested in or knowing about anything but its local
and immediate affairs. Many French-Canadian deputies did
not have the means to be present at parliamentary sessions,
while others were indifferent. The popular leader Joseph
Papineau had to be brought to the Chamber by military
escort, after having been absent from sessions for two
years. Gradually, *habitants* replaced the manor lords as
deputies. Wade tells us that "the latter found refuge in the
executive and legislative Councils and, when they lost the
confidence of the masses, they allied themselves to the
English ruling class."[20] As a defeated people the French
Canadians were spontaneously on the defensive politically;
they found the English party uncompromising about
keeping the best positions for itself. On the whole, the
French-Canadian experience of parliamentary government
was not a happy one. They tend henceforth to use the
parliamentary regime for defending ethnic and cultural
values rather than political and economic principles. Frank
Scott describes the different attitudes of French and
English Canadians towards democracy: "The English Canadian sees democracy as a form of government in which the
people's will is expressed by a freely elected Parliament.
He believes in the vote, in equal rights for men and
women, in freedom of expression and association, in a free
press and in religious tolerance. His democracy is a process
rather than a given social order; it is a method by which
society can be constantly changed and improved. He sees
many antidemocratic elements in Canada and in several
other so-called democratic countries, and would like to
make these elements disappear. The liberal tradition of the
nineteenth century has bequeathed him a fundamental
belief in civil liberties. His attitude results from a deep
suspicion of ecclesiastical or secular authority.

"The French Canadian has had a completely different
experience with democracy. He knew nothing of it under
the Old Regime, and what he has learned of it comes from
his relations with the English. For him then, democracy is
immediately identified with the struggle for his religious

and linguistic rights. He has made use of democracy rather than adhered to it as a doctrine. His Catholic education makes him more aware of his duties and obligations as an individual than of his personal rights, and he is readier to accept a hierarchical order. He therefore insists more strongly on the rights of groups, called in Canada minority rights, than on individual liberties . . ."[21]

We agree largely with what Professor Scott says about the practise of parliamentary democracy in Quebec. As a vanquished, minority group Quebeckers saw nothing in these institutions but a means of protecting the rights of their collectivity. Still, the majority[22] of people who have discussed this problem take it for granted that there is only one kind of democracy, the Anglo-Saxon type, and measure the behaviour of peoples against this standard. Things are not perhaps so simple as that. We are tempted to believe, with René Gillouin,[23] that there are at least two main kinds of democracy, one of English, one of French inspiration. English democracy is, among other things, individualist, liberal, bourgeois, antiegalitarian and in favour of private property, while French democracy is collectivist, authoritarian, popular, egalitarian and against private property. Perhaps it is because of their historical situation that Quebeckers have been led to conceive and practise this second type of democracy, which differs considerably from democracy as it is conceived by English-speaking people.

Some partial researches tend to prove this point of view. Whatever the case, this is one more realm in which French and English Canadians have, since the beginning of the nineteenth century, expressed differing conceptions and practises. When parliamentary government is granted to Quebeckers in 1791, they are a society decapitated of its elite, living for the most part in the country and preoccupied with surviving a ruinous war and conquest. The higher clergy and the manor lords side with the victors, to obtain either freedom of worship or political favours. Menaced by anglicization and assimilation, Quebeckers refuse (or at least their clergy do) the means of education that the English wish to put at their disposal. Another factor soon contributes to the rift between English and French Canadian: economics. Here is how Mason Wade sees this division between the two: "This division along ethnic lines into 'haves' and 'have-nots,' which lasted for nearly a century, arose largely from the fact that the commercial-minded English had the governmental influence and the access to British capital which enabled them to exploit the Canadian commercial revolution, which began with the Peace of 1783 and the coming of the Loyalists . . . The products of farm and forest had become the major staples as the fur trade declined, and this new trade was largely in English hands. Napoleon's Continental Blockade of 1807, which cut Britain off from Baltic timber, was largely responsible for the revival of a commercial imperialism which flooded Canada with British capital. Canada suddenly was linked with the industrial civilization of Britain. The number of ships clearing from Quebec tripled between 1807 and 1810, with every branch of the timber and lumber trade showing a similar expansion. The French Canadians, long largely ousted from the management of the fur trade, had fallen back on the professions, petty trades, agriculture, and unskilled labour. The professional men and tradesmen were not commercial-minded. The *habitants* were deeply traditional; they practised subsistence rather than commercial farming . . ."[24] This long quote from the historian shows us another trait of this folk society: French Canada was in general peopled with poor individuals who practised subsistence farming and minor trades; they showed little openness towards the mercantile spirit, and were content to lead a traditional life apart from the English and the commercialism that their presence impressed on the colony. Here is how Governor Craig sees the situation: "The Bishop, tho' unknown to our Constitution and confirmed, if not appointed, by a Foreign Power, has been suffered to exercise every Jurisdiction incident to the

episcopal functions . . . In truth the Catholic Bishop tho'
unacknowledged as such, exercises now a much greater
degree of authority than he did in the time of the French
Government, because he has arrogated to himself every
power which was then possessed by the Crown . . . With
the Curés themselves, no direct communication from the
Government exists in any shape; a numerous and powerful
body, dispersed in every corner of the Country, and
certainly possessing a very considerable weight and influence with the people, [they] scarcely know, and are hardly
known to the Government . . ."[25]

The British who wanted to exploit the country made
it easy for Americans to enter Lower Canada; they felt
that the new arrivals were "of English stock, professing the
same religion, speaking the same language, and would
therefore be more easily assimilated and would become
better subjects than those which we now possess." This
was not the opinion of the newspaper *Le Canadien,* which
thundered against "the intrusion of a half-savage people,
whose forays are as much to be feared in Canada as those
made formerly by the Goths and Vandals into Italy."[26]

"Cockloft," of whom the historian Mason Wade says
that he "is thought to have been a young Englishman sent
out to Quebec in behalf of the London timber merchants,"
loses patience with the traditional way of life of Quebeckers. He reports that he conversed with French-
Canadian gentlemen who 'regretted the inert disposition of
the 'Habitants, whom they said neither adversity nor
prosperity could arouse from the torpid habits of their
forefathers; that in general they planted no more now,
although every species of provision had risen greatly in
price, than they did four years ago when the trade was
very trifling . . . Their aversion to labor springs from pure,
genuine, unadulterated *indolence.* Give a 'Habitant milk, a
few roots, tobacco, wood for his stove, and a *bonnet
rouge,* he works no longer; — like the native Savage, who
seldom hunts but when driven by hunger.'[27] Wade adds:
"With a mercantilist's regret he noted that the Canadians'

consumption of imports was 'but trifling in comparison to the extent of their country, the 'Habitants in general manufacturing their own clothes, and in winter substituting skins for woolens. The wants of these people are very few; being perfectly free from any desire of luxury or finery. . . .' " "Cockloft" is shocked to find that 'all the boys in Quebec speak English like Frenchmen, and indeed seldom speak it at all, when the French language will answer to their purpose . . .' He observed an 'inveterate prejudice of the 'Habitants against the British . . .'[28]

There is no doubt that Quebeckers had a tendency to remain isolated and to continue to form a very homogeneous population, even during the English regime.

It sounds paradoxical, but the regime of the manor lord was a powerful influence in keeping the French Canadians isolated and homogeneous. The French-Canadian historian Marcel Trudel fully recognizes this fact. In his words, "The manor regime had only a limited success as a system for populating the country, but it did much more than to group individuals around a manor lord on the two banks of the St. Lawrence. The lord determined the framework of French-Canadian nationality and assured the integrity of the population. When the English became masters of the country, they were not free to divide it up as they pleased; they had to take into account the manor geography which formed a compact whole. The manor farms were already peopled; they were functioning units. They cound not be integrated into a world subjugated to 'free and common socage.' The Vaudreuil-Soulanges peninsula was made a part of Lower Canada (instead of making the Ottawa River a natural frontier) because the distribution of population in manor farms did not allow for penetration otherwise. Moreover, it is the manorial system which permitted the French-Canadian population to preserve its integrity for a hundred years in spite of the continuing flood of English immigration . . . There thus developed two worlds within Lower Canada: the world of the manors which the English are reluctant to integrate, and the world of *townships* where the French Canadians do not want to go (at least until 1921). This phenomenon occurred precisely at the time of the great efforts towards assimilation. Suppose for an instant that the manor system had not existed; there would not have been this division of Quebec into two worlds and the integrity of the population would have lost its essential point of resistance."[29] As the author says, the continuation of the manor system powerfully helped the French Canadians to remain geographically intact; this geographical homogeneity has, in its turn, favoured the social and cultural homogeneity of the group.

From the beginning of English rule, the ties between Canada and France become slighter and slighter. When the newspaper *Le Canadien* speaks of Napoleon, in 1808, it calls him an illegal head of France. Nelson's victory at Trafalgar is celebrated in the city of Quebec as a national victory. The French Canadians grow more and more loyal to England, and help the English Canadians to repel the American invasion of 1812. Meanwhile, in the legislative assembly, the battle against the English administration continues.

The Rebellion of 1837-1838

This rebellion is a very important turning point in Quebec's history. It will have long-term effects on the French-speaking population of North America. Since 1791, the former New France has been divided in two: Upper Canada, which includes today's Ontario, is Protestant and English-speaking; Lower Canada is Catholic and French-speaking, its frontiers approximately those of contemporary Quebec. At that time, each part of Canada is provided with parliamentary institutions and is separately administered. Quebec (Lower Canada), as one historian puts it, can believe itself "confirmed in its aspirations of being a national state."[30] In this colony of Lower Canada, what are the forces at play? There is first of all London, the colonial power, which grants parliamentary institutions to the two Canadas, English and French. Like any colonial power, however, it wants to retain the maximum of control while seeming to give the colonials the greatest possible liberty. Because of the American revolution, it grants more liberty to its colony of Canada than the English people themselves possess. The governor-general stands at the top of the political and administrative structure of Lower Canada, representing London. The bottom of the hierarchy is occupied by a chamber of deputies, elected by nearly universal suffrage. Between the governor and the national assembly there are two councils, one executive, the other legislative; they are composed of members appointed by London and by the governor.

"In the first executive council," says Groulx, "of eight members there are four French Canadians and, of these four, one is notoriously anglicized; in the legislative council, of sixteen members nine are English-speaking and seven are French-Canadian. This is a fairly fixed ethnic proportion in the higher sphere of government for nearly half a century. From 1793 to 1823, of thirty-one people nominated to the executive council, twenty-five are of English origin, six of French origin. There is the same shocking inequality among the magistrates."[31] A like documentation prevails with the higher civil service. The national assembly has a majority of French Canadians, but it has, in fact, but little power in the face of an administration which is English from top to bottom. The country is effectively governed by the British who use the manor lords and the Catholic Church as docile instruments. This is the "aristocratic compact," especially designed to thwart the middle class of English merchants and French-speaking deputies. In this compact, the two principal partners are the Church and the colonial government. Dubuc says: "The aristocratic compact was as useful to the one as to the other. The Church would eventually acquire its legal status and would enforce its monopoly of education for many years; it would even come to participate in the colonial administration. Thus the political authority of a Protestant society became the defender of the values and institutions of the Catholic Church, while the religious authorities of French-Canadian society upheld, in the eyes of their flocks, British institutions."[32]

In 1840, Lower Canada contained 500,000 French-speaking people and 75,000 English-speaking people. Each of these two groups opposed its own middle class to the "aristocratic compact." These two elements came to an agreement to combat the colonial power, but for very different reasons. The French-speaking bourgeoisie appears at the beginning of the nineteenth century, to replace the manor lords and businessmen of the old French regime. It is a native bourgeoisie, emerging directly from the *habitants,* and composed of educated men — doctors, notaries, lawyers, surveyors — who take it upon themselves to represent their nation, to which they remain closely attached. Lord Durham describes them: "The most educated people of each village belong in society to the same families and have the same level of birth as the illiterate *habitants* I have just described. They are attached to them by all the memories of childhood and the ties of blood. The most perfect equality always characterizes their relations; the man who is superior by virtue of his education is not separated from the exceptionally ignorant peasant who rubs shoulders with him by any barrier of custom or pride of interest. He thus combines the influence acquired by knowledge with social equality: he then exercises on the people a power not possessed, I believe, by any educated class in any part of the world." The clergy had controlled the Quebec people since 1760; it will now be obliged to take this new secular elite into account, an elite which has come from the parishes of the people. This middle class will soon adopt the ideas of the times — democracy, liberalism, anticlericalism, and thereby oppose the clergy more and more. About 1830 Mgr. Lartigue, the first bishop of Montreal, will lead a campaign against the Patriots who, under the leadership of Papineau, are urging a national struggle against the English oligarchy. What are their objectives? In the national assembly they battle for responsible government, i.e., a government which controls the expenditures of the administration and the appointments to it. Because they fight against England they are known as the "French party"; inevitably, the struggle takes on an ethnic character. In attacking England, Papineau and the Patriots are also aiming at the British people of Lower Canada, especially the merchants of Montreal, a mercantile middle class living off domestic and international commerce. In the struggle between these middle classes, two ways of life, two mentalities and two societies oppose each other. The economic crisis of the 1830's makes the contest bitterer, the stakes higher. "Around 1830," Groulx tells us, "of 8,000,000 acres of arable land in the manor farms, 5,100,000 are occupied. Land becomes henceforth scarcer in the fertile regions like the area around Montreal, where the buildings press upon each other in greater density."[33] London is opposed to the creation of new manor farms. The crown lands where, in the absence of new manor farms, the *habitant* might have been able to establish himself, have become the object of fraudulent grants and speculations on the part of English-speaking people.

The years preceding the insurrections are particularly difficult. According to Fernand Ouellet, "The crisis reaches all the sectors of the economy, even the lumber trade and the shipbuilding industry. The agricultural crisis has repercussions in the cities; the recession in the forest products industry and in shipbuilding creates unemployment." The historian adds that "in 1837 misery and discontent reign everywhere. The slight hopes entertained for the coming harvest are deceived; the situation grows worse instead of better. Moreover, the crisis of 1837 does not concern agriculture only; it is general. Lafontaine writes in February: 'Perhaps the almost universal distress, as much of commerce as of agriculture, has brought discouragement to the hearts of men. I confess that poverty is great and misery complete in Canada.' "[34]

From the beginning of the 1830's, political battles are so severe that the national assembly, dominated by the Patriot party led by Papineau, is in open conflict with the governor and London. Elections and parliamentary crises follow one upon the other. England makes an enquiry. On March 2, 1837, Lord John Russell presents his conclusions. "The Russell resolution," says Groulx, "clearly authorizes the governor to dispense with the vote of the Chamber for the approval of a considerable sum of public monies. The Imperial Parliament takes upon itself to break the strike of subsidies."[35] This act set fire to the powder keg.

Fernand Ouellet writes: "Since 1830 the idea of revolution had spread among a group of militant patriots. Some leaders spoke of it as a future possibility; others believed revolution to be inevitable. However, there was no systematic effort to create a revolutionary type of organization. Following the Russell resolutions of the spring of 1837, which obliterated any hope of success by peaceful means, the Patriot leaders had to alter their strategy and consider revolutionary action."[36]

During the summer of 1837, parish assemblies were organized. The movement was growing. The St. Charles assembly, called the Six Counties Assembly, reached a paroxysm of verbal violence, and plans were formed to seize the country. Fernand Ouellet reports the words of Dr. Kimbert, one of the Patriot leaders: "Once we have taken the river, we will march on Montreal with forty or fifty thousand armed men. All the *habitants* are well armed, have plenty of ammunition and are very determined. After we capture Montreal, we will go and take Quebec City. I have been to St. Charles; no country has ever seen an assembly so determined to get rid of English government."[37]

Government and clergy intervene. The bishop of Montreal, Mgr. Lartigue, publishes an announcement instructing the population not to rebel against the government, and the government issues arrest warrants for the principal Patriot leaders, who hide out in the countryside around Montreal. Military action against the Patriots lasts a month, from November 17 to December 15, 1837. The government takes the initiative; the Patriots are on the defensive. "They foolishly awaited the enemy in improvised camps where they were inadequately sheltered, when they could have acted as guerillas, harrying the enemy on the roads. In 1837 camps or military parades were organized on the Richelieu River at St. Denis, St. Charles, then at St. Eustache in the North. These camps undertook no concerted action, and had hardly any liaison among them. The people of St. Eustache are perhaps an exception; they had a vague plan to raid Montreal while the royal troops were fighting south of the St. Lawrence. Though victorious at St. Denis, the Patriots did not take advantage of their victory by giving chase to Gore's companies, which had been completely routed."[38]

In 1838, the movement is better organized. Robert Nelson makes a "Declaration of Independence" and an offensive is begun; this time the uprising seems better organized. It had been prepared by homeless, bitter and impoverished Patriots; it was supported by a secret society, the "Hunters' Lodges," whose members were scattered in the United States and on the Quebec side of the frontier as well. However, the whole thing collapsed in less than eight days. Lord Durham wrote of the revolt of 1838 that "it would probably have succeeded even without the help from the United States, if the French Canadians had been better prepared and had had more capable leaders."[39]

Autopsy of the Rebellion

In his recent article which I have quoted above, Fernand Ouellet discusses the Rebellion. Supported by many texts and statistics, his analysis shows that this movement is mostly of the people; its national character is undeniable. In a rebellion more national than political, the villain is the English colonial master. In Upper Canada the movement aims at responsible government, but in Lower Canada the goal is national independence. A new middle class, consisting of members of the professions, has defined the French-speaking people as a nation which it proposes to lead; it wants all the power for itself. The enemy is not only London and the clique of colonial administrators, but also the English-speaking middle-class people with their capitalist business interests. As Ouellet puts it, "The real enemy was the English merchant and his allies, the bureaucrat and the immigrant."[40] On the political level, the Patriot party's leaders are inspired by French and American ideologies; they are fighting for liberal democracy. Ouellet defines the Patriots' nationalism as "fundamentally conservative both economically and socially." "Instead of taking on the responsibility for social and economic reform, the professions are usually opposed, unconsciously, to any far-reaching change; they strive to preserve old institutional structures which have been raised to the status of national values. They cannot base their actions on the long-term needs of their society, for they do not go beyond the interest and ambitions of their own elite group."[41] We should not be surprised to find this national middle class defending its own interests; that's an old story. One thing is puzzling, though: when the Rebellion broke out, why didn't the masses produce a working-class movement to challenge the authority of this middle class? Instead, they went along with their leaders, and did not demand the abolition of feudal practises. "In my opinion," writes Ouellet, "there is no long development between 1802 and 1838 to which we could attach the label 'Emergence of a Class Consciousness in the French-Canadian Masses.'"[42] Ouellet quotes a M. de Pontois, French ambassador to the United States, who visited Quebec just before the uprising; M. de Pontois clearly explains: "Canada, or rather Lower Canada has something almost unparalleled in contemporary history: a people exactly what it was a hundred years ago. Time has stood still as far as these people are concerned. The revolutions which have shaken the world have in no way altered their ideas or their habits, and even the Conquest has not made its mark on them. The two races have not mixed, and each has preserved its own idiom. The French Canadians live today as under French rule: they are subjected to the feudal system, they pay the tithe to their parish priests and their manor lords, and in civil actions they follow the common law of Paris. We find the same ignorance and the same uncomplicated ways as in the last century; the same ardent, sincere faith, the same blind submission to the men of religion . . . Still, they are a French people; this is the key to the present situation . . ." M. de Pontois says that it is their national feeling that is motivating resistance to a government *"whose only faults are the drawbacks of the colonial system."*[43] [My italics.]

Here we must criticize our historian. In his social and economic analyses he seems to have forgotten the most universal and decisive fact of all: the domination of the Quebec nation by a British colonial master. This over-whelming fact explains why the national consciousness is stronger than class consciousness. We may deplore the fact that the masses, instead of making a democratic or socialist revolution, choose to follow the middle class which, while representing the nation, also upholds its class interests. Let us not forget, however, that this middle class confronts another middle class which defends both its own interests and the interests of the British Empire as well. Ouellet knows it well. As he says, "In Quebec the middle-class capitalists, the real masters of economic life, are no longer exclusively involved in the fur trade. They have strengthened their position with interests in lumber, shipbuilding and agricultural products."[44] In short, the English-speaking middle class controls every aspect of economic life. We must not forget either that at this time the Quebeckers are relegated to the countryside while the English occupy the cities. "The gulf steadily widens between rural Quebec, controlled by the professions, and urban Quebec, the world of the commercial classes . . . The Union crisis reveals this separation."[45]

Ouellet's reading of the Quebec situation at the time of the uprisings of 1837-1838 is largely what we still find today; it is described in the same way by the Liberal, Trudeau. The most significant reality of Quebec society is ignored, though this reality permeates it. People tend to explain things as if colonization and domination did not exist, as if one were dealing with nothing but economic agents, free to take up the lumber or fur trade instead of vegetating in subsistence agriculture. Ouellet says, "These elites had taught the lower classes to recognize their enemies: the colonial and metropolitan government, the capitalist, the immigrant and, in a word, the *Englishman.* The latter, according to these leaders, was responsible for all the ills suffered by the 'poor French Canadians.' Thus the masses ought to overthrow the government and chase away or kill the English."[46] Let us brutally ask the question: just what does Ouellet object to in this argument? He would probably tell me that it is just nationalism. Many people hold that a nation, though dominated and humiliated, can have only a national, but not a social, awareness of itself, even though a nation exists as a social reality. The elites of subjugated peoples the world over have ever reasoned thus. In Quebec, the elite was conservative; in Czechoslovakia until recently the elite has had a reputation for liberalism. The fact of domination, however, is the same in both cases. In Quebec we see that colonization even prevents the development of a class consciousness in the masses which might oppose the middle-class consciousness. The colonization may be over sixty years old as in 1837 or over two hundred years old, as it is today; the fact of domination is in no way altered. Clearly, the nationalists who are more liberal or socialist in their outlook must struggle against those who are less so, or appear to be. It is equally plain, though, that they must first all work together to put an end to foreign domination. Ours is the only country where the elite is ticklish on this point. What socialist did not follow Churchill in his struggle against the Germans? *After* the war, the socialists defeated him in a democratic election. Today, as in 1837, when "in big business circles there was violent opposition to the Patriots,"[47] the business elements are against the liberation of Quebec. Only men have a country; money has none.

With the defeat of the Rebellion of 1837-1838 and the Act of Union which followed, an era draws to a close: the era of an oppressed ethnic group which dreams of becoming free one day. In his post-mortem on the Rebellion, written in 1839, the journalist Etienne Parent wrote: "There were people, and we were among them, who thought that with the support and the favour of England, the French Canadians could flatter themselves that they were preserving and expanding their nationality so that they might be able, later on, to form an independent nation . . ."[48] As Fernand Dumont puts it, "The Rebellion marks the defeat, in a sort of agony or death throe, of this first attempt to define the situation and the future of the French-Canadian nation."[49] This despair of the defeated has never been better expressed than by François-Marie Thomas Chevalier de Lorimier, a notary and married man with three children, who was to be executed in 1838:

"May my execution and the execution of my gallows companions be of use to you. May they show you what you can expect from the English government. I have only a few hours to live, but I wanted to divide this precious time between my religious duties and my obligations to my fellow countrymen. It is for their sake that I am dying as an infamous murderer on the scaffold; for their sake I have given up my wife and children . . . and for their sake I die crying: 'Long live Liberty! Long live Independence!' "[50]

Chapter 4
The Quiet Conservatism of a Colonized People

The French-speaking bourgeoisie which controlled the Quebec Assembly in the years 1820-1840 behaved like a national bourgeoisie, assuming the task of defining the Quebec community and its future. A nation was struggling for its independence. The people were not very responsive to the political ideas of this bourgeoisie, but many supported the plan to liberate Quebec. As a group, the clergy remained faithful to the British Crown. Derbishire, an envoy of Durham, reported this remark of Abbé Ducharme, parish priest of St. Thérèse: "It was the educated men, the doctors, notaries, and lawyers, who were at the head of the rebellion and were the great seducers of the people, and he [the abbé] seemed to derive from it an argument against educating the lower orders."[1] With the Rebellion crushed and its leaders in exile, the clergy could recover its influence over the people with the help of the British government. Thanks to Governor Durham's activities as spokesman for Quebec, the British authorities became aware of the situation prevailing there.

Durham states that he had come to Canada expecting to find a conflict between the people and the executive, but instead of that he found "two nations warring in the bosom of a single state: I found a struggle, not of principles, but of races . . . The national feud forces itself on the very senses, irresistibly and palpably, as the origin or essence of every dispute which divides the community; we discover that dissensions which appear to have another origin are but forms of this constant and all-pervading quarrel; and that every contest is one of French and English in the outset, or becomes so ere it has run its course."[2]

Durham's remedy is simple: he suggests that Lower Canada, mostly French-speaking, be assimilated into Upper

Canada, mostly English-speaking. "I entertain no doubt of the national character which must be given to Lower Canada; it must be that of the British Empire; that of the majority of British America; that of the great race which must, in the lapse of no long period of time, be predominant over the whole North American Continent. Without effecting the change so rapidly or roughly as to shock the feelings and trample on the welfare of the existing generation, it must henceforth be the first and steady purpose of the British Government to establish an English population, with English laws and language, in this Province, and to trust its government to none but a decidedly English Legislature."[3] Durham adds: "I should indeed be surprised if the more reflecting part of the French Canadians entertain at present any hope of continuing to preserve their nationality. Much as they struggle against it, it is obvious that the process of assimilation to English habits is already commencing. The English language is gaining ground, as the language of the rich and of the employers of labour naturally will."[4] Durham could hardly be franker.

Resulting from the Rebellion, the Durham Report and the Act of Union are a watershed in Quebec's history. From the ideological point of view, this is the most significant period till the end of the 1950's, over a century later. One cannot overemphasize the importance of this era. The middle-class professionals of Quebec have emerged from the peasantry, and they support the kind of traditional culture which has developed in Quebec since the Conquest. Is it by choice or by necessity? The professionals are the elite of a people economically, socially, and politically dominated; this elite is obliged to defend what exists, namely a people relegated to agriculture. Quebeckers do not support their traditional type of economy by choice; the dialectics of the situation compel them. The middle class wants to lead the people to independence with the help and favour of England, but this people is, for the moment, made up of poor and illiterate farmers. In resisting the oppressor and the English-speaking mercantile group that represents him, the national middle class defends a life style created by the Conquest and the failure of the Rebellion. We have no reason to believe that the middle class is primarily interested in preserving this way of life; it is above all insisting on the right of the Quebec people to a life of its own as a complete society. Papineau and his followers demand liberty for a majority group which has been militarily, economically, and politically subdued by a minority.

After 1840 the picture changes completely. Even the most committed French Canadians are filled with despair. Their task is no longer to lead their people to independence, but to struggle against assimilation and anglicization. Some, like Etienne Parent, former partisans of Quebec independence, learn to change their tune. In 1839 he writes: "We have always believed that our 'nationality' could only be maintained with the sincere tolerance, if not the active assistance, of Great Britain. Now they tell us that rather than help us to preserve our nationality, they will work openly to destroy it root and branch. We French Canadians are so situated that our only alternative is to resign ourselves with the best possible grace . . ."[5] With the support of Durham, the clergy becomes the chief spokesman of the Quebec people; it will define an ideology of preservation rather than an ideology of independence. This new ideology about to be expounded is a tragic step backwards. Well aware that they are soon to become a minority group, Quebeckers will strive not for independence but for the preservation of their culture. The French Canadians are no longer a nation which must one day acquire independence, but an ethnic group with its own special culture (religion, language, customs); it will preserve this culture as a sacred heritage. Durham accused the Quebeckers of having neither history nor literature, and their task is to show him that they indeed have a past, and a noble one; down with the privilege of those appointed to define our lives for us!

On the banks of the St. Lawrence, as later in Acadia, the English soon realized that they had to divide the Quebeckers among themselves in order to foster a viable State which they might run as they pleased. Lord Elgin knew this when he wrote: "Until the French break into political Parties and join British Parties with corresponding names, I do not think any strong and lasting administration will be formed . . . The national element would be merged in the political if the split to which I refer was accomplished."[6] Dumont writes: "Politics becomes a field where politicians defend their nationality from time to time, but it is only one of many areas where nationalistic ideologies find expression."[7] Responsible government offers professional people opportunities for employment and for some vertical mobility in the civil service and business worlds. Georges-Etienne Cartier, businessman and politician, is one of the first examples of the kind of Quebecker who could profit by the new scheme of things. He participates in the Rebellion of 1837, but, as Wade put it, "he took no part in the second rising, having perhaps been led by his lifelong Sulpician friends to see that the clergy was right in condemning opposition to the constituted authorities, a view which he later recognized as 'the only one that offered some chance of salvation for the French Canadians.' "[8] With the support of this same clergy, he and his party will win all the elections in Quebec right down to the end of the century. Conservatism is triumphant. Young people will leave the cities to live in the country, the heartland of the traditional culture. Gérin-Lajoie's novel *Jean Rivard* vividly expresses this glorification of the soil. In 1849, the author writes in his journal: "I am planning to go and live in the country as soon as possible . . . Ah! If only I were a farmer! They do not get rich by impoverishing others, as lawyers, doctors, and merchants sometimes do; they obtain their wealth from the earth, a condition which seems *the most natural* to man. Farmers are the least egotistical and most virtuous class of the population, but they need educated men to look after their interests. The educated farmer has plenty of leisure to do good; he can be a guide for his neighbours, advising the ignorant and championing the weak against the rapacity of the speculator. The enlightened and virtuous farmer is, in my opinion, the best sort of man."[9] Some of the novels of this period are constructed around the theme of loyalty to agriculture and ancestral values. These romantic works, as well as historical studies, propagate the conservative ideology which will be more systematically developed by the Church and the middle class.

The historian Michel Brunet writes: "The French-Canadian Church henceforth enjoys a liberty it had never possessed since 1760. Without being entirely aware of it, the Church benefits from the establishment of pastoral responsibility and of a new climate of religious tolerance in the Protestant elites of Great Britain and English Canada . . . From 1840 to 1865, the French-Canadian bishops undertake a Catholic counterreformation. This action was necessary, as freethinking had made much progress in the secular ruling classes, and the population at large had fallen into the habit of neglecting its religious duties . . . The clergy wages a vigorous campaign against the last representatives of free thought. Opposition to the campaign comes from the French-Canadian Institute and from all the anticlericals who have remained faithful to the revolutionary romanticism of the 1830's. They have no influence on the masses."[10] The English have given the Church a free hand in return for its loyalist stance during the Rebellion; this liberty is used to take the people in hand, an enterprise which succeeds completely. From this time on, the Church's role in Quebec's national life is the same as it is in many minority groups: it provides compensation. According to the Church, the people of Quebec should not be too disheartened by their present status as a minority group, for their rewards will come later; Quebeckers should not try to imitate the material success of the

English, but should endeavour to fulfill themselves, to become what they are. What if they are beaten and impoverished? Providence has given them a mission to accomplish in North America: to evangelize and civilize the continent.

The national historians, especially Garneau, help the Church to create the new conservative ideology. Though raised on Voltaire and Raynal, Garneau recommends caution and respect for tradition: "In our case, a part of our strength lies in our traditions; we stick to them or change them but gradually. The history of our own mother country gives us many examples to follow . . . We do not wish to claim as great a destiny [as hers], but our wisdom and our unity will greatly diminish our difficulties and excite the interest of the nations, who will thereby look upon our cause as more holy."[11] The "Catholic Reaction"[12] (an expression coined by Father Léon Pouliot, S.J.) took a few years to eliminate every element of anticlericalism in Quebec. The clergy's greatest battle was against the French-Canadian Institute, whose members were freethinkers. Auguste Viatte describes the struggle: "The final battle approached. Quebec City was coming around, but Montreal had become intractable. The French-Canadian Institute was attacking the Church, and Mgr. Bourget wanted to have done with it. In 1857, a priest went to the Rolland bookstore and destroyed 1500 volumes placed on the Index, among them the complete works of Lamartine, because they included *Jocelyn* and *The Fall of an Angel*. In 1858, the bishop imposes a similar auto-da-fé on the Institute." Arthur Buies makes a last stand with his *Lantern*. "He peddles his newspaper himself, but in vain; the stores refuse to carry it, and the last number appears in March 1869. Garneau is dead, Crémazie in exile; it's the end of an age. Springtime breezes give way to drought, so prolonged that it lessens the fertility of the soil and alters the climate."[13] Buies lasted until 1869, but the *Catholic Reaction* had already achieved its goals many years before; the Church had taken the bulk of the population in hand.

According to Dumont's interpretation, the Church acquires its predominance with the consent "of leaders, even unbelievers, who clearly saw that religion was an essential factor of social solidarity and a fundamental part of the French-Canadian nation as distinct from the English."[14]

The federation of Britain's North American colonies becomes a constitutional reality with the British North America Act; this scheme fosters lines of development laid down by Durham and the Act of Union. In 1840, the Act uniting English-speaking Upper Canada and French-speaking Lower Canada was supposed to bring about the rapid anglicization of Lower Canada; this was the general idea propounded by Durham and the English jurists. The project backfired, but with Confederation, i.e., the union of four British colonies in North America (Upper Canada, Lower Canada, New Brunswick, Nova Scotia), the progress of assimilation seemed irreversible. Quebeckers, a minority in the new political formation, clung even more tenaciously to their defensive and conservative ideology. The French Canadians were a majority in Lower Canada but not in Canada as a whole. Even in Quebec, where they represented about 75 per cent of the population of 1,000,000 or so, their economic and social position did not reflect their numerical importance. The big cities like Montreal and Quebec City had a majority of French-speaking people, but the English predominated in commerce, industry, and finance. Even in Quebec itself, French and English Canadians are at the time opposed in everything: the French Canadians are poor rural folk, Catholics, and French by language and tradition; the English Canadians are urban dwellers, much better off economically, and Protestant.

Confederation introduces an era of great economic development for Canada as a whole, but Quebec's economic uneasiness forces many people to emigrate to the United States. The centre of Canada's economy shifts from

Quebec to southern Ontario, and Quebeckers are forced to seek work in New England. To counteract this emigration, the clerical elite and the middle class start a large-scale movement of colonizing and of return to the soil. Quebec continues to develop the conservative ideology which encourages it to remain inside its frontiers: "Relatively sheltered from Anglo-Saxon influences, Lower Canada is absorbed in maintaining a personality it wants to make immutable, in a closed universe outside of space and time."[15] Quebec grows more and more distant from France. In the year of the Paris Commune, 1871, Mgr. Raymond writes: "The capital of France, the centre of this iniquity and uncleanliness, seems to me a godless land, like unto Babylon or Sodom, calling down upon itself the vengeance of Heaven."[16] The theory of the two Frances is gradually developed; Thomas Chapais gives the most explicit formulation of it: "At the present time there are two Frances, the radical France and the conservative France, the France of unbelievers and Catholic France, the France that blasphemes and the France that prays. The second France is our France."[17] This estrangement from France is not counterbalanced by any reconciliation with the English-speaking people of Canada. In the 1880's, the Riel affair further strains the relations between Quebec and the rest of Canada. With a Quebecker, Laurier, as prime minister of Canada from 1896 to 1911, there appears to be a truce between the two groups; Laurier owes his election as much to Quebec as to the rest of Canada.

During Laurier's tenure of office the Quebec economy expands rapidly. Although the process of industrialization was mostly directed from outside, introduced into Quebec by the English-speaking element, the first decades of this century see a radical transformation of Quebec's traditional way of life. Quebec first encounters the effects of massive industrialization through the problem of the working class.[18] There too, conservative ideology plays an important part. To prevent Quebeckers from joining international labour unions, the clergy contributes heavily to the establishment of Catholic unions, designed to protect the workers from the religious neutrality of the Americans.

When Laurier leaves the government in 1911, after fifteen years in power, Quebec has greatly changed. In 1871 the population was 80 per cent rural; forty years later it is half urban. Montreal's industrial and commercial development attracts many rural people, who swell the numbers of labourers and wage-earners. The English-speaking minority still possesses the wealth and the industrial and financial power. Even in those days Errol Bouchette, a Quebec public relations man, is strongly advising his countrymen to get into industry rather than farming; for him, the future of Quebec is industrial rather than agricultural. Bouchette notes with bitterness that a French-speaking population of 1,293,000 sends only 722 students to university, while the English-speaking people of Quebec send 1,358 students out of a population of 196,000. There are only twenty-seven French-speaking students in science, compared to two hundred English-speaking students. Viatte writes: "Around 1890 French-Canadian literature seems on the point of dying. Conformism becomes immobility; all novelty is censured." Critics vainly deplore "this quasi-inability to produce which results from language difficulties, the absence of institutes of higher learning, the rarity of books, the general indifference to any elevated subject, desperate politicking and the progressive invasion of the American spirit."[19] A few years later, in the first decade of the twentieth century, the Montreal literary school inspires great hopes. However, the principal members of this school apply themselves only to the minor literary genres and do not relate their criticism to the social and economic facts of domination. As a result, their activity does not square with reality. Another forty years will pass before a literary revival meshes with a growing national and social consciousness.

At the time of the Boer War of 1899, a conflict arises between French and English Canadians, because the Quebeckers refuse to participate in England's imperialist war in South Africa. This dispute is revived during the Great War of 1914-1918. The Ontario separate schools question further aggravates the strife between Quebec and Canada. In the midst of war the province of Ontario, which has a substantial minority of French-speaking people, takes reprisals against the French Canadians, who don't want to go to war in Europe on behalf of England. Ontario passes Bill 17, which is intended to banish the French language from its schools. This statute embitters the relations between Quebec and the rest of Canada. In the national assembly of Quebec, in 1917, a cabinet minister tabled a bill intended to bring about the withdrawal of Quebec from Confederation; after several days of debate, he finally withdrew his bill. The premier of Quebec, Lomer Gouin, took a stand against withdrawal from Confederation, invoking the fate which would be reserved for the French-speaking minorities of Canada; he also stated that a separate Quebec could not survive economically. In this period Henri Bourassa, grandson of Louis-Joseph Papineau, the leader of the Rebellion of 1837, becomes the champion of a kind of pan-Canadian nationalism; he argues for a Canadian rather than a British foreign policy. About 1917, apparently disillusioned by the direction of events — conscription for overseas service, harassment of French-speaking minorities in Ontario — he turned to the study of religious problems and published a book entitled *The Pope, Arbiter of Peace,* and gave an important lecture on "Language, Guardian of the Faith." He had a profound influence on generations of Quebeckers; this influence explains some of the positions taken by the traditional nationalists who gravitated around *Le Devoir* and *L'Action nationale.*

In the early postwar years, industrialization in Quebec develops at an ever more rapid pace. The United States steadily increases its economic and cultural control over

Quebec. In 1921, the French-speaking population of Canada reaches its lowest level, 27.9 per cent of the total population. The urban population of Quebec reaches 51.8 per cent, exceeding the rural population for the first time in history. Montreal has 618,506 inhabitants, of which 63.9 per cent are French-speaking. Several important industrial centres develop: Three Rivers, Hull, Shawinigan, Grand-Mère, Chicoutimi, La Tuque. Foreigners continue to exploit the natural resources of Quebec. Lack of capital and of native technicians aggravates the domination of the country. In the 1930's a separatist movement develops as a direct continuation of the traditional nationalist movement. The war put an end to this movement, though the conflict between French-speaking and English-speaking people did not diminish; as in 1899 and in 1914-1918, the majority of Quebec's French-speaking people were opposed to sending troops overseas. The Second World War brought on further industrialization and urbanization, thereby assuring Quebec of a turbulent future.

Confrontation and Catching Up

When the Second World War broke out in 1939, the dominant ideology in Quebec was the conservative dogma which began to develop in the second half of the nineteenth century.

Of those who had assumed the task of defining the nation, of orienting its collective action, the majority had rallied to this ideology. In the century, more or less, that the conservative ideology was dominant, it was championed by the clergy and many members of the professions. This was not the only definition of Quebec that existed in this hundred-year period, but the other definitions did not find favour with the public and did not influence the behaviour of most Quebeckers. The clergy and the professions who, for all intents and purposes, controlled most of the information media, the schools, the books and the textbooks, had all the time in the world to disseminate this ideology. French Canadians living in another political unity, Canada, could if necessary forget the fact that they were Quebeckers and go along with the ideology of Canada. Quebeckers could escape, physically or otherwise, from their nationality and live as if they were Canadians or North Americans. This is precisely why ideological disputes did not arise in this period. Moreover, as long as the national education remained in the hands of the clergy, they could propagate and impose their vision of Quebec society. This vision defines the Quebeckers as a group possessing a culture, i.e., a group which has a noble history, which has become a minority in the nineteenth century, and whose duty it is to preserve the heritage which it has received from its ancestors and to transmit this heritage intact to its descendants. The essence of this heritage is the Catholic religion, the French language, and an indeterminate number of traditions and customs. This vision looks to the past as the perfect time. When this ideology was created, French Canadians were becoming a minority and were in danger of assimilation. Naturally, this doctrine enshrines the traits of Quebec society during the second half of the nineteenth century; this society was in fact Catholic, French-speaking, agricultural and traditionalist. Menaced by assimilation, it rigidified, retaining its essential characteristics unchanged. This rigidity was rationalized and justified; to its apologists, this culture was not only the birthright of every French Canadian, but the best of all possible cultures. These ideas became dominant over the years, during the nineteenth century, and were transmitted almost intact up to the beginning of World War Two.

Gérald Fortin, a Laval· University sociologist, has analysed one of the principal reviews which transmitted the conservative ideology over many years: *L'Action française,* later called *L'Action nationale.* He has analysed it from its appearance in 1917 up to 1953.[20] The main motifs of the conservative vision are found there; the review extolls the merits of the French language, the

Catholic religion, spiritualist culture, national history, rural living, the family; it warns against the dangers of English imperialism, industrialization, urbanization, and mass communications media; it recommends that people buy Quebec products and show respect for the two cultures and for French-speaking minorities. In its last decade, 1943-1953, *L'Action nationale* begins to take an interest in economic and social questions; the working-class problem makes its appearance in its pages. Fortin writes: "As regards the ends and means of the ideology, we can see that the goals have not changed; they were even more strongly emphasized when new interpretations of the situation appeared."[21]

After World War Two, the conservative ideology is contested by other elements of the population: trade unionists, intellectuals, journalists, artists, students and some members of the professions. This kind of opposition certainly has historical antecedents; it can, in many ways, be related to the liberal tradition. It does not deny that Quebec possesses a culture different from that of the other people of Canada, a culture whose main features must be preserved; it holds, however, that this culture must be brought up to date. The movement which develops after World War Two is above all an attack on the old conservative vision. Its negative part, the criticism of the old ideology, is the most developed; the positive part is below the waterline, as it were; it is almost always implicit.

Quebec's old ideology and power structure had become obsolete because of demographic, economic, and social changes during the war; the old order takes on an air of unreality. In the decade 1939-1950, for example, the number of manual labourers in Quebec is doubled. According to a study by the economists Faucher and Lamontagne, "this increase, in absolute terms, is equal to the growth witnessed during the whole century ending with 1939." The authors add: "During the period under review, the rate of industrialization in Quebec has been higher than that of Canada as a whole. Since 1939, in volume terms, output of manufacturing industries rose by

92 per cent in Quebec and by 88 per cent in Canada, while new investment in manufacturing increased by 181 per cent in this province and by only 154 per cent in the whole country."[22] Nathan Keyfitz shows how Quebeckers have shifted from agriculture to industry: "During the war and post-war years, the population in agriculture in the province of Quebec dropped from 252,000 to 188,000, a decline of 64,000. This decline more than counterbalanced the steady rise that had been shown from 1901, and hence the surprising result that, although the province of Quebec is almost three times as great in population in 1951 as it was in 1901, it contains fewer men in agriculture. The increase in non-agricultural industry is shown in every one of the thirteen main occupational groups, except fishing and trapping which, like farming, declined sharply. The rise from 79,000 to 237,000 in manufacturing occupations is especially conspicuous."[23]

It seems that Quebec underwent a more massive transformation in the years 1939-1949 than in any other decade of its history, except for the Conquest and the Rebellion. Industrialization and urbanization finally swamped the conservative view of things, which had successfully resisted them up to that time. On the level of everyday life, indeed, the dominant ideology had been ineffectual for many years. It still guided the nation's politics, but no longer inspired the actions of Quebec's more dynamic individuals, who either kept to themselves or joined small groups which were operating within other terms of reference. The patriotic societies continued to defend French-Canadian culture (religion, language and traditions) while most people shared a certain number of images of Epinal[24] concerning their nation; others became ideologically integrated with other North American societies, Canada particularly.

After the war, the battle against the old ideas begins in earnest. During the late 1940's and the 1950's, the movement's best-organized headquarters is the social sciences faculty of Laval University (sociologists and econo-

mists). Reviews like *Cité Libre* attach themselves to this
nucleus along with movements like the Canadian Institute
of Public Affairs, whose members include intellectuals,
professors, trade unionists, journalists and liberal politicians. These movements and individuals are inspired by
their social and economic analyses of Quebec and by their
knowledge of other Western democracies; they undertake a
systematic criticism of Quebec's conservative ideology and
culture.

In the 1950's social problems are attacked, i.e., the
problems of the working class are recognized. Even
L'Action nationale, long a leading exponent of the
conservative viewpoint, introduces so-called social themes
in its pages. The Asbestos strike of 1949 had already
caused great upheavals; people began to realize that
Quebec society was no longer a traditional society based
on agriculture but a society in which the majority of the
citizens were wage-earners; some years later, it will be
observed that Quebec society had gradually become
proletarian.

From today's perspective, the Asbestos strike of 1949
is one of the decisive events that makes possible the
springtime of Quebec. Quebec workers, employees of a
foreign company, the Canadian Johns-Manville Co. Ltd.,
go on a wildcat strike before all the tricks of conciliation
and arbitration can be brought into play. Led by the
reactionary Maurice Duplessis, the Quebec government
sides with the American company. "On May 5 a Provincial
Police convoy, twenty-five cars and a towtruck, left
Sherbrooke for Asbestos, to bring the strikers to their
senses. Twenty-five workers were arrested. After their
arrest, the strikers were brought to the Iroquois Club for
questioning. Various methods of interrogation were used:
kicking, beating with nightsticks, punches, slamming
people against walls. Many of those released had swollen
faces and other signs of the beatings they had received.
The police threatened to arrest them again if they did not
go back to work the next day. These brutal scenes aroused

the indignation of the archbishop of Montreal, Mgr. Joseph Charbonneau, who supported the workers. A few months later, the prelate was ordered to a retreat, where he might meditate upon the disadvantages of encouraging strikers."[25]

The Asbestos strike has all the main features of the Quebec drama: foreign capital; a liaison between the Quebec government and foreigners; the Church in its habitual role of docile partner to the political and economic power in its exploitation of the workers. In 1949, the Church and the intellectuals both took the side of the workers.

In criticizing Quebec's conservative dogma and culture in general, opponents of this ideology had to criticize not only ideas, values, behaviour and institutions, but also groups and often individuals who were responsible, in their opinion, for the general orientation of Quebec politics. This line of thinking brought the critics to consider the role of the clergy, which had always been in control of the national education. We can say that those years saw the birth of a freewheeling discussion of education, religion, and the traditional interpretation of national history.

Inevitably, the critics came to attack Quebec Catholicism and those who had narrowed it and made it peculiarly "Quebeckish." Maurice Tremblay has well expressed this situation: "The Church has adopted a fiercely defensive attitude towards the influences of Protestantism and French modernism, and has thereby succeeded in keeping French-Canadian culture wholly Catholic. Unfortunately, we must confess that this victory was largely won at the price of a narrow and sterile dogmatism, and an authoritarianism fixed in a conservative mold. This French-Canadian Catholicism seems to us, on the whole, a conservative Catholicism, in the rearguard of the radical transformations which world developments demand of Christianity . . . We have here an example of that narrow and unproductive ultramontanism which the Church has used as its chief weapon in its general policy of conservatism, and in the defense of French-Canadian Christianity." The

Church had always joined forces with that traditional society which the conservative vision (for which the Church was itself mostly responsible) wished to preserve in a North American world which denied it and surpassed it on every hand. As Tremblay writes: "As a rule, the Church in French Canada swims against the flood tide of industralization and urbanization. It tries to preserve the life styles and social categories of a rural civilization which it could dominate and inspire with that ideal of the religious Christian life for which it has a great nostalgia."[26]

The new critics who are redefining the terms of life in Quebec have another favourite target throughout this period: the political power of the *Union Nationale* party and of its leader Maurice Duplessis, in office from 1936 to 1939 and from 1944 to 1960. Relying on the rural population and on the numerous priests who controlled it, this party put into practice the conservative doctrines which had existed in Quebec for many years. Totally pragmatic, suspicious of intellectuals and ideologists, Duplessis espoused the most conservative of politics in the name of Quebec autonomy and peasant good sense. In the highest style of traditional conservatism, he favoured a personal politics in which everyone knew his place; in which the prince distributed largesse to the good folk — the ones who had voted for him — and let the bad folk — the counties and regions which had showed him some opposition — go rot. His methods of running Quebec were as outdated as the ideology which inspired him; these methods had many features of a preindustrial society, which agreed perfectly with the conservative dogma, which in turn had been created expressly to assure the continuation of the traditional society which Quebec had been in the middle of the nineteenth century.

The liberal opposition was made up of Liberal party members and other opponents of the regime; it took them fifteen years to defeat the two powers, political and ideological, which had fused together, which complemented one another, and which enjoyed the favour of the

majority of voters. The traditionalists relied on two basic
characteristics of the Quebec situation: first, the conviction that Quebeckers have a unique identity which sharply
distinguishes them from other North Americans; and
second (a corollary to the first), the belief that Quebeckers
had remained a people with a traditional culture even
though they were living in a largely industrialized and
urbanized society. In short, the ideological opposition
before 1960 wanted to bridge the gap between Quebec
culture (ideas, values, symbols, attitudes, motivations) and
Quebec society (technology, economy, urbanization, industrialization). This gulf between Quebec culture and
Quebec society was creating a complete alienation of
Quebec from other North American countries. Thus, in the
period 1945-1960, the opponents of the regime in Quebec
(its ideology and political power) were inspired not only
by an ideology of confrontation but more fundamentally
by an ideology of catching up.

Realizing that Quebec was far behind in almost every
field of human activity, the opponents of the status quo
attacked especially the elites which they considered
responsible for this sad state of affairs. What new Quebec
were the critics searching for? What kind of society did
they want it to become? At this stage the critical and
negative part of the program was quite naturally the most
developed and systematic. The conservative vision and the
political power had so idealized Quebec culture that the
critics felt compelled to begin by deflating some of the
balloons which had filled up over the years. According to
the establishment, Quebec had the best system of education, the purest religion, the most refined language and the
most humanistic traditions. Such ideas inspired some with
a missionary's eagerness to share these cultural treasures
with the rest of the world. According to an idea attributed
to Duplessis, Quebeckers had become improved Frenchmen. It is not surprising that the first task the postwar
opposition assigned itself was to criticize what Quebec had
become and to confront the phantasmagoria of its elites

with the sordid truths of reality. The positive aspect of this ideology of confrontation was much less clearly articulated.

The critics agreed on what they were opposed to but not on the goals of the society they wished to construct. They were perhaps too preoccupied with their struggle against the authorities to worry about the positive aspect of their beliefs. Individuals and groups with widely varying backgrounds had joined forces against the regime: Catholic and international trade unionists, Catholic leaders, progressive and Catholic intellectuals, factions of anticlerical and socialist groups, members of the Quebec or federal Liberal party and students at various levels of their scholastic career. It is no exaggeration to say that because of Quebec's history and its intellectual and political climate, only one reasonably clear model of an alternate society suggested itself to the critics: the model of the other North American societies. What most of them wanted was a liberal democracy for Quebec, like that of Washington or Ottawa. Some of them were influenced by currents of thought in Europe, France especially — as expressed in the review *Esprit*, for example — but the majority looked, consciously or unconsciously, to the Ottawa model. In this period, some professors and students of the Laval social sciences faculty were open supporters of Ottawa. The most typical example is Maurice Lamontagne, who rallied to Ottawa in 1954 and was joined a few years later by three important leaders of the postwar opposition: Marchand, Pelletier and Trudeau. Several became civil servants in the federal government. During the 1950's several were against the Ottawa regime, but with the virtues of hindsight we can say that they unconsciously favoured the liberal democratic model which was the source for much of their positive ideology.

Today we can easily recognize that most of the reformers and critics of the 1950's implicitly honoured the Ottawa model. They wanted Quebec to imitate it and to become fully integrated with the rest of Canada, while preserving some original cultural features. Pierre-Elliott Trudeau, for example, is today prime minister of Canada; Pelletier and Marchand are members of his cabinet, and Maurice Lamontagne, formerly a federal minister, is now a senator. There are other old reformers, too, who now revolve in the federal government's orbit.

Since 1840 three ideologies have appeared in Quebec. The conservative ideology is the assertion that Quebec must preserve its national culture. The ideology of confrontation is a vehement denial of the previous century's conservative ideology, and in its positive aspect, for a long time merely implicit, Quebec's aim is to catch up with the liberal democratic system of the other North Americans. A third ideology has developed in the last ten years: the affirmation of Quebec society by development and by participation; it is the negation of the negation represented by the second ideology of confrontation and catching up. As far as means are concerned, this third ideology resembles the national ideology of the Patriots of 1837-1838: it is militantly in favour of independence for Quebec.

Chapter 5
The Springtime of Quebec

Since the end of the Second World War, Quebec's traditional elites — the professional people and the clergy — have been bitterly criticized, as we have seen, by new social strata aspiring to power. The painter Paul-Emile Borduas publishes his manifesto in 1948; its very title, *Refus global* (Total Rejection), symbolizes the attitude of a whole new generation. These criticisms and rejections will appear regularly for a whole decade.

On the other hand, the very personification of feudal conservatism and sordid jingoism, Premier Maurice Duplessis, is reelected in 1951 and again in 1956. During this entire period, he asserts that Quebec is autonomous; at the same time he is giving away the natural resources of his country to American capitalists, and for practically nothing.

Thus, in the early 1950's, he grants a Labrador iron mining concession to an American corporation in return for a royalty of one cent per ton of ore extracted. We know that in the same period Newfoundland is receiving thirty-three cents a ton from a similar operation in the same region.[1]

A sharp conflict arose between the Confederation of National Trade Unions and Duplessis, who wanted to bring the trade unions to heel. Many segments of society — universities, reviews, intellectuals, trade unionists — were fighting the power of Duplessis and the Catholic Church. The *Union Nationale* party pursued a very conservative political line, but still made some improvements in the country's infrastructure: roads, schools and public buildings. In his battle with the cities, Duplessis depended on the farm vote, and he therefore favoured the country areas with progressive agricultural policies like rural electrification and farm credit. In his external policies he waged a merciless war against the Ottawa government, which he accused of all-out centralization. In his campaign against the federal government, he demanded a greater effort from his political machine, which brought him victory at the polls from 1944 to 1960.

In 1953, Duplessis appointed a Royal Commission to study the constitutional problems of Quebec. Made up of right-wingers and traditional nationalists, the Tremblay Commission took the kind of tone and reached the kind of conclusions that pointed to a growing awareness, on the part of the Quebec people, of its true conditons. It seemed likely that the Quebeckers would insist on a redefinition of their province's constitutional powers in future. In the social and economic spheres, the Tremblay Commission hewed closely to the traditional doctrines of the Church and its encyclicals.

This period of cultural strife lasted from 1948 to 1960, and prepared a comeback for the Liberal party, which was finally elected to power in 1960. The death of Duplessis in September 1959, in the far North of Quebec, had greatly contributed to the Liberal victory. His successor, Paul Sauvé, had begun some legislative and administrative reforms, but he also died before the elections of June 1960, after one hundred days in office. And so, after an eclipse of nearly twenty years, the Liberals led by Jean Lesage were returned to office.

This was no ordinary election, but rather what sociologists call a total social phenomenon — something more than a transfer of power from one party to another, like the elections in a good Anglo-Saxon type of democracy. This election implicated all of society, affecting every part of it; it called in question established power and conventional wisdom. It marked the end of a period in Quebec's history, and the beginning of an era which many a French Canadian believed would lead his country to a greater political autonomy, or even to complete independence.

The best-informed elements of the population were extremely eager for change and renewal. As a result, the Lesage government felt the electorate would go along with the reforms it had announced in its political platform. The Liberal campaign slogan had been: "We must have change!" After 1960, the "Quiet Revolution" began.

What was this quiet revolution? Who but Quebeckers could dream up such an idea, or carry on such a thing as a quiet revolution? The concept unites the hot with the cold and makes them work together. Our people, in fact, have a "hot" culture, i.e., a Dionysian culture that has been repressed, historically, by the domination of frigid influences (the French metropolis, the British, the Americans, Jansenism and religious rigidity). How strange, then, after centuries of subjection, that enough "hot" elements have survived to make us refer to a simple reform movement and a climate of change as "revolutionary." Seized with remorse and, apparently, not wishing to seem boastful, we cooled down the hot word "revolution" by coupling it with the cool adjective "quiet." The alternation between hot and cool plays an important part in the collective psychology of Quebeckers, not only because of the climate but because of the coexistence of two cultures of which one is renowned for its cool, understated character. A few years ago, a song called *"Le Rapide blanc"* rose to great popularity, not only in Quebec but throughout French Canada; its words and music were based on this alternation of hot and cool.

The Quiet Revolution saw whole classes of people "take the floor," people who had never before spoken for themselves, but had let the clergy and the professions be their spokesmen. From 1960 on, the "quiet ownership of Truth," which Lesage himself called a French-Canadian characteristic, was violently questioned by the new elites. The Quiet Revolution was more a mental liberation, a development of critical attitudes towards men and affairs than it was revolutionary action per se. It was, above all, a reevaluation of ourselves, a reappearance of a spirit of independence and of enquiry which had been smothered in the snows of the hundred-year winter. Quebeckers grew confident that they could change many things if they really wanted to. They began to shrug off the fatalism of a conquered minority who had come to think that they were born to lose, that they were far from having the capacities of a Papineau.

The Quiet Revolution inspired a criticism which gradually turned from internal self-examination to an analysis of external factors: the British, the American . . . We quickly learned to give them their share of responsibility for the inferior status of French Canadians, after one hundred years of Confederation. In the 1950's, ever the good-humoured colonized people, Quebeckers criticized themselves; from 1960 on, they became painfully aware of the blatant contradictions of their society. The year 1960 became a symbol of unblocking, of openness, of liberation. The Quebec springtime, the springtime of nature, of green trees and flowers in bloom, arrived as suddenly as the political and intellectual thaw of 1960. A day before Quebec was still cold, stifled, petrified; then it was warm, open and teeming with life. The French Canadians had abandoned appearance for reality. 1960 marks the beginning of their reconciliation with themselves. Leaving behind them the 1950's, when a vengeful self-criticism was the order of the day, Quebeckers recovered their self-confidence and began to ask themselves what else they could accomplish as a community. For a century they had striven to preserve their heritage; more recently, they had tried to catch up with the other North Americans; now they asked themselves if they did not have some original contribution to make to the world of human societies. They were reasserting their vocation as a nation. Spring brought with it the memory of an old dream, older than the Act of Union of 1840 — the dream of that Rebellion for which at Pied-du-Courant, twelve French Canadians died whose names are engraved in history. Some time was still to pass before this dream reached the general public and the political parties . . . and came to haunt the easy conscience of the colonial masters.

For the time being the Liberal party, victorious on June 22, 1960, did its utmost to modernize the State and to accomplish its program of reforms. These were relatively timid undertakings, no more than any honestly progressive administration on this continent would think of doing. The ideas and perspectives of the Lesage government were not very far removed from those of any liberal administration. For a Quebec which was emerging from the Middle Ages, this was already a giant step forward. Everybody, or almost everybody, was delighted; Canada itself was in a festive mood, for its elites felt that Quebec was finally coming of age and was about to become "a province like the others." The federal Liberals, whose leader Louis St. Laurent had already declared that Quebec was "a province like the others," were exultantly congratulating themselves that a former federal cabinet minister had become the premier of Quebec. At the beginning of the Quiet Revolution, the best political experts felt that Quebec's future was finally settled and that the province was falling into step with the rest of Canada. The most unrealistic of the experts even began to think that Quebec could lead Canada along a path of reform. The most romantic already saw Canada as a bilingual country.

They soon changed their tune, for events were about to take an entirely different direction. Far from becoming "a province like the others," Quebec became more and more a province not like the others. The most astute Quebeckers began to wish that Quebec were not a province at all. Little by little, the Quiet Revolution turned into the "Quebec question." The English-speaking Canadians were soon to ask, "What does Quebec want?" The French Canadians, astonished by their own audacity, did not know what to reply.

To get into power, the Quebec Liberals had been forced to be as favourably disposed towards autonomy for the province as their old rival of the 1950's, Maurice Duplessis. They realized that the patriotic and autonomist spirit of the French Canadians was not dead, and that it would be only by taking this fact into consideration that they could hope to get themselves into office again. The party, though frankly pro-Quebec, was fully aware of the modernization program it had to undertake. Two important changes gradually occurred. First of all, Quebec stopped looking upon itself as a culture, i.e., an ethnic group with a language, a religion, and a set of values different from the other groups in Canada, and began to see itself as an industrial society of the twentieth century. Secondly, the Golden Age was no longer to be looked for in the past but, as in other industrial societies, in the future. In retrospect these seem to be the two most significant changes of the early 1960's.

When French Canadians began to see themselves as an industrial society rather than as an ethnic community, they initiated all the difficulties which were to appear in the traditional relationship between Quebec and Canada. Since Confederation, Quebec had considered itself a special group within a Canadian society; in 1867 it formed the Dominion of Canada with three partners, but in 1948 it found itself with nine partners, nine other provinces which, with Quebec, formed the political entity called Canada. When Quebeckers began to question the old ethnic definition they had given themselves, they also implied a criticism of the political society they had lived in since 1867.

The 1960's witnessed a growth of separatist movements which had already appeared in the late 1950's. Even the party in power, led by a federalist, adopted an increasingly autonomist stance. Though elected by the new middle classes, by the English-speaking people of Quebec and by the business community, the government had inspired hopes of changes in many sectors of the population — intellectuals, students and the young in general. Increasingly, it favoured more autonomy for Quebec and forced the federal government back on its last resources. In 1962, having implemented several progressive programs in the social and economic fields, having appointed a Royal Commission on Education and expanded Quebec's activities in the French-speaking world, the Liberal party was reelected with the slogan "Masters in Our Own House." One of the planks of the election platform was the nationalization of the electrical utilities. The Liberals, by this slogan and this election platform expressed the wish of an ever greater number of Quebeckers to take possession of their economy and to control their political destiny. A new vision was arising to replace the conservative ideology which had been dominant up to 1945. This vision was the logical outcome of the ideology of confrontation and catching up which appeared in the late 1940's and made possible the Liberal victory of 1960. Since that time the people of Quebec had lived in a climate of intense ideological conflict. Rather than political parties, social classes and splinters of social classes determined the boundaries of ideological dispute. Ideological differences were also, to a great extent, a reflection of a generation gap.

The adherents of the third ideology were mostly separatists, but separation was not their primary concern. Independence was not so much an end in itself as a means of creating a more just and humane society. There was no assurance, in fact, that the majority of separatists were not as conservative as the federalists; colonization transmits and imposes habits of thought so compelling that colonized man imitates the colonial master even in the domains where he opposes him.

Only the ideology of catching up is by definition federalist, for it envisages the pure and simple integration of the Quebec people in a greater American world, through the intermediary of Canada. It is essentially a negation of Quebec as a nation. A recognizable nation is an adventure in communal living which relates to a set of specific cultural phenomena exhibiting stable characteristics over time, e.g., language, behaviour, customs, traditions. The most powerful bond uniting the members of such a nation is, as Renan puts it, "the desire to accomplish great things together." The federalists recognized the importance of this tie because they hastened to ridicule such aspirations on the part of the Quebec people. Of the three ideologies which were wooing the *"habitants"* at that time, only the ideology of catching up was not nationalist.

The Failures of the Quiet Revolution

The revolution weighed anchor and sailed off on a sea of ambiguity: was it the last flicker of national consciousness or the first step on the road to freedom? From the beginning, Quebec politicians played constantly on this ambiguity, inevitably perhaps, given the situation. In any case, it was not a very effective strategy. Sometimes, beneficial policies were announced with grand reassurances to everybody: the English Canadians, the Americans, the capitalists, the Ottawa set. On other occasions, ultimatums were hurled and the outsiders were threatened with a terrible retaliation, but when the time came to act, not much was done. The slogans of our politicians were a good illustration of this mentality. "Not necessarily independence, but independence if necessary" was one catchword; another was "Equality or independence." These men seemed to have taken lessons from General de Gaulle. Morbidly sensitive to public opinion, for they had no very definite programs, they almost all lived on the short-term credit of parliamentary debates. When the Quebec Liberals, for example, felt that their accomplices in Ottawa were in a weak position, they got tough with the federal government. When, however, the Ottawa people got back their nerve, the Quebec group played along with them.

What was the main theme of the Quebec political scenario? The national assembly was still largely controlled by old village politicians who had served their political apprenticeship in the 1940's and 1950's. A majority of them were completely outdistanced by the activities of the most dynamic members of the community: trade unionists, young people and intellectuals. The politicians had created symbols, initiated policies, and raised hopes that the most recent generations of Quebeckers had taken to heart. The young people wanted to see these new directions come to fruition. The politicians often seemed unable to keep abreast of the times.

Confronted with the difficulties of a policy aimed at reforming their society, Quebeckers took evasive action in the form of a great leap backwards. Was it due to electoral politicking or to the ingrained responses of a colonial people? In any case, everything seemed to grind to a halt. We seemed to be back in the pre-1960 era, the heyday of purely verbal battles with Ottawa. The Quiet Revolution had already shown signs of running out of steam in 1964 and 1965. In the elections of June 1966, power fell to an ill-equipped team which could boast few competent individuals. A number of very valuable specialists were suddenly out of office, and a new period was ushered in, a period of uncertainty and inaction. With the *Union Nationale* party in power, the Liberals began to repudiate their own works, and to become once more the time-serving federalists of yesteryear. Their leader Lesage was soon on the scent of a new odour in politics. The meteoric rise to power of the old Quebec opposition — Trudeau, Marchand, Pelletier — had brought some precious allies to the English Canadians, who would soon mount a large-scale offensive against any attempt by the people of Quebec to loosen the federal grip on their country. The Quebec Liberals sniffed at this new breeze, which promised to help them sail back into power. Trudeau, who was negotiating to establish diplomatic relations with the Vatican, would be able to deliver them, on a platter, the heartfelt gratitude of a majority of Quebeckers. St. Peter had once sold out for much less!

The team of Lesage and Laporte had not awaited these signs from Heaven to take a hard line against those colleagues who still believed in the springtime of 1960. They repudiated the constitutional scheme of Gérin-Lajoie and expelled René Lévesque from the party. These two politicians had been the chief architects of the Quiet Revolution.

In 1967, de Gaulle lent his prestige to the Quebec cause; his cry "Long live Free Quebec" (*Vive le Québec libre*) was heard round the world and created diplomatic tensions between Ottawa and Paris. Daniel Johnson seemed to have trouble keeping up with what was going on, and appeared embarrassed by de Gaulle's friendliness towards Quebec. Right up to his death, Johnson continued to give reassurances to both parties to the conflict.

In June of 1968 the English Canadians realized that Trudeau was the man to bring Quebec to heel and voted overwhelmingly in his favour. The French Canadians went along with the trend, giving in to their old mania for self-flagellation, and elected a great majority of Liberals to represent them in Ottawa. Johnson died the following autumn and Bertrand, the number two man in the *Union Nationale* hierarchy, succeeded him as leader. Bertrand continued to reassure everybody, but the job was too much for him and he had to be hospitalized. The quiet counterrevolution continued.

The daily newspapers gave the impression that the springtime of the early 1960's, which had promised a warm summer, had been prolonged unduly, that from time to time there was still a touch of frost, here and there. Was winter perhaps returning? The *Parti québecois* was prepared to answer that question.

The Parti québecois

Since 1960 a number of separatist movements and political parties had emerged in Quebec; some survived, others disappeared. The most important party, the R.I.N. (*Rassemblement pour l'Indépendance Nationale*, Assembly for National Independence), had a considerable impact on the public and at the polls. In the elections of 1966, it broke into provincial politics with about 8 per cent of the popular vote. Considering our electoral laws and our political habits, this was no mean success. The R.I.N. had disseminated the ideas of independence throughout Quebec, and since 1960 had done battle on all fronts. In November 1968, René Lévesque, the former provincial Liberal cabinet minister, formed a new separatist party, and the R.I.N. agreed to merge with this ambitious new movement. The *Parti québecois* combined all the separatist parties in one organization. Unlike the other political groups which were militating for Quebec's independence, this party organized itself in the hopes of attaining power; it was more than simply a political education movement. Moreover, because it seemed to draw its supporters from every level of society and from every part of the province, the *Parti québecois* could speak to all the people of Quebec, unlike the R.I.N. (too exclusively intellectual and urban) and the *Ralliement national* (too strongly rural). By drawing these two parties into its orbit, the *Parti québecois* became the most important separatist political organization since the Patriot party of the 1830's. Faced with the appearance of this party, the traditional Quebec parties were perhaps thinking of a coalition, while their younger members were perhaps considering the possibility of joining the *Parti québecois*.

Ottawa's Counterattack

Trudeau's rise to power in Ottawa was the federalists' most spectacular reply to the separatists, but the central government had been actively working against separatism many years before the appearance of Trudeau. In July 1963, well aware of the seething discontent in Quebec, the Canadian government, in the best British tradition, appointed a Royal Commission "to enquire into and report on the present state of bilingualism and biculturalism in Canada and to recommend what measures might be taken to ensure the development of Confederation according to the principle of equality between the two founding nations, taking into account the contribution of other ethnic groups to the cultural enrichment of Canada, as well as measures to be taken to safeguard this contribution."

The Commission has been at work for nearly eight years. It has published a preliminary report and a volume on the languages spoken in Canada. In 1965, in their first public document, the commissioners opined that "Canada, without being fully conscious of the fact, is passing through the greatest crisis in its history." Curiously enough, Quebec is no exception to the rule; as in every colonial situation, the dominant power is always behind the times, and unaware of how conscious its subjects are of the society that is made for them. For a century, French-speaking people have fought for an acceptance of bilingualism by the federal government. If Ottawa had become aware of this problem before, events might have taken a different course. The federal government was prepared to accept bilingualism only at a time when Quebeckers, declaring themselves a majority in their own country, were taking on attitudes and political stances which went far beyond bilingualism. As in every other colony, it's a case of too little or too late. The problem that interests Quebeckers at the moment is the question of monolingualism in Quebec; the bilingualism that Quebeckers had frequently demanded for Canada as a whole no longer seems a worthwhile goal to many French Canadians.

Let us recognize clearly, here in Quebec, that when the members of any group — nation or class — are subjugated to another group, and see that they are considerably weaker than their masters, they ask only for equality. When the dominated group becomes more and more aware of its strength and the balance of power seems to shift in its favour, it demands all the power and all the culture for itself. This is plainly what is happening in Quebec today.

Chapter 6
Liberty vs. the Dollar

Ever since the idea of independence arose in Quebec — according to Professor Séguin[1] it is almost two hundred years old — many arguments have been preached in its favour. They change from one period to the next, as do the arguments against independence. In the last ten years, we have gone through all the arguments for and against separatism; some have been added to the ever-growing list. Curiously, the number of arguments against independence has steadily diminished. Some time ago, the federalists settled solely upon the argument from economics. According to them, an independent Quebec is not a viable economic entity. The Prime Minister of Canada is almost the only person who wants to justify Canadian federalism by other than economic arguments; we shall examine his arguments later on. For the moment we shall content ourselves with a résumé of the separatist arguments. In the following chapter we will deal with the federalist theories of the Prime Minister.

In 1966 André d'Allemagne, one of the founders of the R.I.N., published a book entitled *Colonialism in Quebec (Le colonialisme au Québec).*[2] This book summarizes, as I see it, the bulk of the separatist arguments. It is the most lucid and comprehensive indictment of Confederation that has ever been made.

Political Colonialism[3]

The political life of Quebec is full of colonial symbolism, starting with the lieutenant-governor of Quebec, who represents the Queen of England: "Laws are sanctioned, cabinet ministers appointed, and court summonses served in the name of the Queen. The members of parliament and civil servants must swear allegiance to her.

Registers of births, marriages and deaths are addressed to her. Court sessions at every level open with a cry of 'Long live the Queen,' and nobody can begin an action against the Crown without permission."[4] Colonial folklore gives rise to such absurdities as this: the Gentleman Usher of the Black Rod, a kind of parliamentary majordomo, is literally known in Quebec, d'Allemagne tells us, as *"le gentilhomme huissier à la verge noire."* Other aspects of the colonial situation, alas, are not as harmless as this. "The federal government has exclusive control over money, banking, credit, customs, 'national' defense, communication and transportation at the interprovincial level, the criminal code, and citizenship. It has the upper hand in the areas of immigration, taxes and foreign trade, and also has some say in the areas of natural resources, social security, and culture and education."[5] The central government retains the lion's share of revenues, so that Quebec is continually obliged to borrow in the money markets; where honest reform is concerned, Quebec's street of broken dreams is named Bay — or Wall. In the capitalist world of North America, English-speaking financiers and Ottawa politicians are as thick as thieves; they control political administrations for the greatest good of the economic system. The same people often show up in financial organizations and in political parties. In the Liberal convention of 1968, most of the candidates for federal party leadership were millionaires in their own right. For them, Quebec is a kind of subprefecture whose least impulses to freedom must be controlled. A French-Canadian economist has thus summed up the historical position of Quebec: "Are we to believe that, since 1867, every provincial government has systematically lied to the Quebec people in promising them large-scale reforms in the administration of their country? Or are we, on the contrary, to think that our provincial governments have always been prevented from realizing their programs because Ottawa prevented them, and especially because foreign financiers refused them the means to accomplish the necessary reforms? The Uncle Toms that Ottawa and the continental financial interests tolerate in Quebec dare not go beyond the few liberties that they are permitted."

For a long time, the colonial masters have fostered political parties molded on the parties of the metropolis; these parties have welcomed both masters and slaves into their ranks, encouraging them to undertake actions in common. This is an extremely effective way of giving the slaves the illusion of having a say in the running of their country. They thereby forget their oppression. Historically, the key posts in these parties have gone to the property-owning and middle classes. "The national bourgeoisies, once they have emerged, are only opposed to the imperialistic domination in a hesitant and inconsistent way, because of the connections some of these people have with the imperial power; they are also afraid of setting in motion social forces which might prove uncontrollable."[6]

Social Colonialism

The Quebec nation, because of its colonial status, could not develop normally. "Nationalism itself has helped to inhibit social conflicts; oppressed as they were, the people of Quebec were afraid that internal divisions would erode their position even further. 'Cease your fratricidal strife' was the reply to the few nationalists who demanded social reforms. Thus Quebec's traditional nationalism has usually been reactionary and asocial, in which it differs from today's 'neonationalism.' " D'Allemagne, the author of the above quote, asserts that the *Rassemblement pour l'Indépendance Nationale* had become "the most socially advanced party in Quebec, in Canada, and no doubt in North America."

The problems of the French-Canadian workers themselves have never been the central concern of the Quebec trade unions, whether they were affiliates of American unions, like the Labour Federation of Quebec *(Fédération des Travailleurs du Québec),* or under the thumb of the

Church, like the C.S.N.[7] As a result, the trade unions have never become fully aware of the double alienation of Quebec workers: national alienation and socioeconomic alienation. "Under Duplessis, the 'old' trade unionists fought stubbornly and sometimes heroically for the recognition of workers' rights, in the face of a regime which was allied to big business and opposed to the interests of the workers. These men unconsciously associated any form of nationalism with the regime which, in fact, exploited national feelings while receiving support from the colonialist press, foreign financiers and big businessmen."[8]

Cultural Colonialism

In the separatist indictment of Confederation and colonialism, the state of the French language in Canada is exhibit A. Language has always been the main cultural difference between the Quebeckers and their colonial masters, and every generation of resisters has been deeply concerned about it. D'Allemagne is no exception; for him, widespread colonialism in Quebec has reduced the French language to a pitiable state: poverty of vocabulary, anglicisms, syntactic and semantic contaminations and a slackening of articulation in pronunciation. These are the blemishes one usually finds in the speech of French Canadians.

The British North America Act, the fundamental constitutional law of Canada, established bilingualism in Quebec to protect the English-speaking minority. In the federal sphere, the two Houses must also use both languages. In practise this arrangement makes Canada a monolingual state, but turns French-speaking Quebeckers into bilingual people by necessity. Quebec's English-speaking people have no reason to learn French. French in Canada has the same status as those who speak it — the status which accrues to an impoverished, oppressed and colonized people. For d'Allemagne, "cultural colonialism is simply a result of economic and political colonialism."[9] "The colonial master exercises his cultural sway through the organs of the mass media, which belong to him and do his bidding."[10]

For some years now, especially since Jacques Berque published his ideas on the subject, many Quebeckers have come to realize that socioeconomic imperialism alters not only the language of the oppressed people, but their whole culture and personality as well. As d'Allemagne puts it, "An oppressed people has no chance to be involved in the great realities, the great problems and the great decisions of life. Such a people can hardly help but express themselves badly; after all, what have they to express . . . except their solitude or their rebellion?"[11]

The French-Canadian poets have felt most deeply, and best expressed, this cultural alienation; we could quote almost any of the poets who have recently begun to emerge from their prisons of silence to make themselves heard in the world. Jacques Brault, one of the most representative of them, writes: "Quebec does not exist. It is still nothing but a passion, a disease to be cured or — better — a promise to keep . . . It's only a dream, a desire; we want it in spite of all our weaknesses, in spite of all opposition. When I go out in the world, when I leave the everyday life of my native village behind me, I find I can only speak of Quebec in the past or future tense. I may talk to a fellow Quebecker and he may talk to me, but each of us remains alone in this meeting in present time. One cannot speak of Quebec in the present tense; Quebec is not in the world because Quebec is not itself; yet if it exists somehow, this existence can be only an *existence apart*."[12] Paul Chamberland makes a lucid diagnosis of the Quebec situation when he says: "We simultaneously endorse two value systems, and we try to live with both of them. More precisely, we want to believe that these value systems can be reconciled to one another; in fact, they contradict each other. We want to resolve the contradictions, and we are unaware that to realize this project would be to achieve our own destruction."[13]

On the subject of cultural alienation, d'Allemagne draws the following conclusion: "Colonialism reduces the culture of the colonized person to the level of folklore and propaganda."[14]

Economic Colonialism

One does not have to be a Marxist to recognize the importance of economic factors in social life. An examination of the political, social and cultural forms of colonialism in Quebec leads, in the final analysis, to the brutal fact of economic colonialism. In the debate between federalists and separatists, economic arguments have a very important place. We can go so far as to say that the federalists' last line of defense is the proposition: "An independent Quebec would not be a viable economic entity." This thesis is supported by a host of eminent economists. Let us begin by noting that there are very few economists in North America who do not favour the status quo. In Marx's day, the economists had already become the loyal watchdogs of the bourgeoisie. This does not imply that the economists are necessarily wrong when they examine the Quebec scene from the economic point of view. Some of them, the Liberal party's financial critic for example, add that questions of independence and liberty are not settled by statistics. In any case, the economic argument concerning Quebec is skillfully wielded by the defenders of the status quo, from the chambers of commerce to the federal cabinet ministers. Most of Quebec's leading economists join in this chorus.

Economic arguments are so popular with federalists, you'd almost think the French Canadians really benefited from Confederation, that their economic situation would be threatened if they withdrew from it. Oddly enough, statistics published by the federalists themselves tell us a very different story. The Royal Commission on Bilingualism and Biculturalism went beyond its original mandate, quite right in its belief that there had to be economic reasons for the inferior status of French-Canadian language and culture. Economists reported to the Commission on these matters, and their findings were supposed to be published in 1969, or whenever the time was ripe. *La Presse,* a big daily newspaper in Montreal, in fact the biggest French-language daily in North America, published extensive excerpts from the Commission's report before it was officially released. The information contained in it was not, strictly speaking, a revelation. We knew, approximately, how low the French-Canadian economic status was. The federal documents described this state of inferiority with numerical precision. Below are some of the significant passages from these "revelations."

Mme. Lysiane Gagnon, who wrote the *Presse* preview of the B and B report on economic life, summed up the results of the federal enquiry as follows: "French-Canadian enterprises in Quebec are small in scale, produce little, pay low wages and involve traditional industries, i.e. the oldest ones, closer to cottage industry than to modern processing industry: sawmills, tanneries, etc. Their market is local, provincial at best. Again in Quebec, foreign enterprises (those whose stock is at least half owned by nonresidents in Canada, usually Americans) have the opposite characteristics: large-scale production, high productivity and good wages. They are technically perfected processing industries with a high export volume. English-Canadian enterprises are situated halfway between these two categories."[15]

Canada is economically dominated by the United States. Quebec, however, is dominated not only by the United States but by English Canada as well. Thus English-Canadian enterprises live off the leavings from American industry, and French-Canadian enterprises live off the leavings of the leavings. The *Presse* analyst gives the gist of the Commission's report: French-Canadian enterprises are systematically rated as inferior in relation to their type, the salaries they pay, their volume of production and the markets they reach. Mme. Gagnon says on the subject of markets that "the foreign enterprises in Quebec are far ahead with 51.5 per cent of the total exports from the province, followed by the English-Canadian companies with 44 per cent. The French-Canadian businesses trail badly with only 4. 5 per cent of the export market."

French-speaking Quebeckers in Business

Concerning the place occupied by French-speaking people in businesses in Canada and in Quebec, Lysiane Gagnon reported in *La Presse* of October 23, 1968, as follows: "Within the big Canadian manufacturing industries, French-Canadian personnel become less and less numerous as one goes up the corporate hierarchy; in passing from the category of hourly wage-earners to that of management, the proportion of French Canadians dropped by two thirds. To each 'majority' there corresponds a different 'minority.' "

To make a comparison, in Canada (excepting Quebec) less than 5 per cent of the management men are French Canadians, although French Canadians constitute 10 per cent of the workers. In Quebec (excepting Montreal) 30 per cent of the managers are English-speaking and they hold 80 per cent of the top positions; the same group supplies only 7 per cent of the workers.

In Montreal, 60 per cent of the workers are French Canadians, but this group holds only 17 per cent of the management jobs; the rest are held by English-speaking people.

More than four out of five managers earning more than $10,000 a year are English-speaking, and only one in five of these is required to be bilingual.

Of the French-speaking managers, seven out of eight work in companies owned or controlled by English-speaking people.

In Quebec, the local population provides the blue-collar workers, but three-quarters of the jobs paying more than $15,000 a year are held by managers from the

English-speaking communities of Montreal, from the rest of Canada and from the Anglo-Saxon world in general.

The French-speaking people of Canada have traditionally been treated as "hewers of wood and drawers of water." The jobs they hold have changed somewhat since the industrialization of Quebec, but it appears that they have not acquired much more status in the new hierarchy of employment than they had in the old.

A Doubtful Bilingualism

In a *La Presse* headline of October 24, 1968, we read: "Bilingualism is a one-way street and English is the working language [in Quebec itself] in secondary industry."

French Canadians employed in Quebec's secondary industry for the most part use English on the job.

Outside of Montreal, over 96 per cent of French-speaking managers are required by their contract to be bilingual. On the other hand, half of the English-speaking employees are not obliged to know French.

In Montreal this pattern is even stronger: 86 per cent of English-speaking people earning more than $5000 a year know only English.

Even blue-collar workers have to adapt themselves to a foreign language. Most English-speaking foremen do not know French, and notices for the employees are usually written in English.

French-Canadian university graduates are for all intents and purposes nonexistent in technical fields (engineering), research and development, and are concentrated in the public relations area, in an intermediate position between the English-speaking management and the French-speaking workers.

Why French-speaking People Are Inferior

The *Presse* headline of October 25, 1968, was

" 'Competence' does not explain everything; there is the danger of 'assimilation.' " Here is Mme. Gagnon's résumé of the last part of the B and B report on economic life:

"How can we explain the fact that so few French Canadians obtain important management posts in private enterprise? There plainly is a barrier somewhere. This barrier results more from a cultural factor than from deficiencies in ability or in training.

"The young French Canadian who contemplates a career in industry finds himself in a dilemma. He feels that to be successful he will have to sacrifice a part of his linguistic and cultural identity. This man feels profoundly alienated." He sometimes gets the impression he is betraying something: "Should the French-speaking people take the interests of the company to heart and become totally integrated with it, this would entail, they feel, the danger of 'selling' their individual identity, and their collective responsibility to the society and the culture in which they were born."

In fact, half the French-speaking management personnel in big companies think that a French Canadian who is successful in a large corporation "is more English than French," and 45 per cent feel that a French Canadian who has had several promotions in a large English-Canadian enterprise "is bound to protect the interests of the English Canadians" against the interests of the French Canadians.

Most of the university graduates in commerce, science and engineering pursue careers in the Quebec civil service or in private practise rather than in big business.

There are cases of flagrant discrimination, but many corporations are prepared to hire competent French-speaking people for key management jobs on three conditions:

1. The candidate for the job must have a perfect command of English;

2. He must agree to accept job transfers outside of Quebec;

3. He must function within the company in the

same way as his English-speaking colleagues, i.e., he must for all practical purposes think and act in English.

Finally, even if the French-Canadian manager agrees to all these implicit conditions, he is doubly handicapped in his efforts to work his way up in the corporation. He is bound to encounter many obstacles arising from the fact that he has a French-Canadian background, and these difficulties are likely to have a baneful effect on his morale, making him less efficient on the job and thereby compromising his chances for promotion.

The Quebeckers' Humble Lot in Life

The table below brutally exposes the economic conditions of French-speaking Quebeckers.

Mean Annual Income of Wage-earning Males in Quebec by Ethnic Origin in 1961

Ethnic Origin	Income in Dollars	Index
Total	3469	100.0
British	4940	142.4
Scandinavian	4939	142.4
Dutch	4891	140.9
Jewish	4851	139.8
Russian	4828	139.1
German	4254	122.6
Polish	3984	114.8
Asian	3734	107.6
Ukranian	3733	107.6
Other European	3547	102.4
Hungarian	3537	101.9
French	3185	91.8
Italian	2938	84.6
Indian	2112	60.8

Source: Canada Census 1961, special compilation

The French-speaking people of Canada, who are referred to in orations as one of the founding nations, have incomes amounting to 80 per cent of the income enjoyed by the other founding nation, the English Canadians. In their own country, Quebec, the land they discovered in the sixteenth century and began to settle in the early seventeenth, their average per capita incomes as a group "amount to 65 per cent of the average per capita incomes of English Canadians" (*La Presse*, October 26, 1968).

In the last thirty years, the situation has deteriorated. In 1930, Quebec residents of British descent had 3.3 per cent more people in the professions, management and business than the per capita average for the population as a whole. In 1961, this group was 8.7 per cent above the provincial mean.

Quebeckers of French descent have sunk more than 1 per cent further under the provincial mean in the last thirty years, and are now more than 2 per cent under-represented in the occupations with highest income.

At the other end of the occupational spectrum, where skilled and unskilled workers are concerned, the positions of the two groups are reversed. In thirty years, the number of workers per capita in the group of people of British descent has dropped to 6.4 per cent below the provincial mean; the French-speaking group has remained about 0.7 per cent over-represented in these categories.

In other words, while the English Canadians were climbing Quebec's social ladder, the French Canadians were going down or staying where they were — on the bottom.

Moreover, *for any given level of education, French Canadians earn less than all other ethnic groups.* Lysiane Gagnon quotes federal government economists on this topic: "French Canadians benefit the least from education. They obtain even fewer economic advantages than the Italians in their progress from elementary school to high school to university . . . the French Canadians would be perfectly justified in showing less enthusiasm for education than other ethnic groups" (*La Presse,* October 25, 1968).

The distribution of jobs is also less determined by language than by ethnic origin. Of the people in Newfoundland of French origin, 85 per cent report their native language as English (as do 65 per cent in British Columbia, 57 per cent in Nova Scotia, 55 per cent in Prince Edward Island and 50 per cent in Alberta). In spite of these variations, the relative economic standing of French Canadians is the same from one province to another, from one ocean to the other.

The articles in *La Presse* conclude: "A man remains a French Canadian long after he has abandoned the French language. Although a large number of French Canadians outside of Quebec are already assimilated (because English is their native language), they remain, as it were, marked men, and usually have the kind of generally inferior jobs that unassimilated French Canadians have" (*La Presse,* October 26, 1968).

Faced with these facts and statistics thus revealed by a federal enquiry, we might well ask whether the economic argument, so dear to the advocates of the status quo, still has any validity. Investors are certainly worried by the *idea* that Quebec could become independent. "Investment," they say, "requires a stable political climate." What they mean is: a colony is a colony; the day it becomes independent, it will threaten their capital and their projects. A few years ago, a French-speaking underling candidly admitted on the national television network that his bank had received telephone calls from New York about a declaration made by the premier of Quebec concerning the presidential form of government. The New Yorkers were upset and were wondering if Quebec was going to become independent in the near future. The bank reassured the American financiers that it was nothing but a lark. A colony is a colony. After two hundred years of conditioning, who but a fool would dare to think otherwise? Nevertheless, independence is the burning question in Quebec today. The French Canadians are beginning to realize that they are the community of "white niggers of America." This is no enviable fate, but should independence make their lot even harder, it would be even less enviable. Federalist and capitalist propaganda inspires the French Canadians with a continual fear of degenerating from "white niggers" to "black niggers" should they separate. All the good apostles of federalism are suddenly full of love for the people, for the common flock which the bad shepherds would lead to an even greater misery.

Chapter 7
The Right of the Richer

In the preceding chapter, we have considered the arguments usually invoked in favour of independence, and found them to be of several kinds: political, economic, social and cultural. In all these domains, Confederation seems to have been a bane to Quebeckers, who find that after a century of this regime their national culture and native language are severely menaced; and that in the working world, they occupy, even in Quebec, a position inferior to the English Canadians and to every immigrant group with the exception of the Italians (perhaps if the recent Italian immigration to Quebec had been considered, the Italians themselves might have been placed ahead of the French-speaking Quebeckers, who constitute 85 per cent of the total population of Quebec). Their economy is also for the most part controlled by English-speaking foreigners, American and Canadian. In every other province of Canada, the French-speaking groups are losing ground and are rapidly becoming anglicized, except in those areas immediately adjacent to Quebec, where the pace of assimilation is much slower. Finally, the separatists argue that there is such a thing as a Quebec nation, and that this nation wants to live its own life and to develop in its own way.

The supporters of the status quo have far fewer arguments to offer, and in the course of time they have tended to be reduced to one: an independent Quebec would experience a sharp drop in its standard of living. On a continent which rightly prides itself on this standard of living, the argument is an important one. The federalists, aware of this, have become habituated to levelling it at all opposition. It has become the sole, the prized piece of artillery in the Ottawa arsenal. Fortunately, we are no longer subjected to the sort of ludicrous remarks that

Sabrevois de Bleury addressed to Papineau in 1839. We follow Hubert Aquin in looking upon this Sabrevois as the distant ancestor of all of today's federalists. To defend the colonial regime, he used arguments that nobody would dare employ today, even though the English throne is occupied by a woman, as in 1839. Sabrevois rebutted Papineau in these terms: ". . . the throne had come to a young princess, a woman whose beauty was such as to win every heart, but your heart was steeled against every sentiment of nature. Simple courtesy was foreign to it, and the only honours you saw fit to proffer our gracious Sovereign were the licentious comments of a vulgar tongue, the sort of language none would dare to use towards the meanest of women."[1] No federalist would now use such arguments. Today, however, the French Canadians have more important things to do than insult princesses.

Today the economic argument reigns supreme. Since the revelations of the Royal Commission concerning the economic status of French Canadians, however, many have asked themselves whether the benefits of Confederation have not been somewhat exaggerated. Unless we believe that without the English Canadians to employ them in their industries, the people of Quebec would have let themselves starve to death, it is reasonable to ask if they might not have been better off without the English-speaking people.

The federalist cause is fortunate to have a prestigious advocate in the person of the Prime Minister of Canada, the Right Honourable Pierre-Elliott Trudeau. An economist and a lawyer, he combines in his person all the qualities one could hope for in a Canadian who would be neither English-Canadian, French-Canadian, Ukrainian-Canadian nor anything other than purely and simply Canadian. Independently wealthy, very well educated, of mixed ethnic background, perfectly bilingual, he can transcend the ethnic peculiarities which afflict almost all of humanity to become a type of *homo sapiens* whose numbers, alas, are all too few in Canada. As Prime Minister of this Confederation, he is particularly well placed to favour an increase in the number of people who are free from every ethnic antagonism. A fierce defender of federalism, he adopts the style of a Savonarola in his withering attacks on patriotism and nationalism, and uses the cold logic of a St. Thomas Aquinas to develop his learned demonstrations against the independence of Quebec. The garden-variety federalist uses only economic arguments in his attempt to persuade Quebeckers to remain in the "Dominion of Canada." The Prime Minister, however, employs a panoply of arguments and writers which, though it may not win our immediate support, reveals the immense erudition of the author and the qualities of a Julian Benda, of a great scholar who has nothing but sarcasm for patriotic humanity, and devotes all of his energies to the study of eternal values. Trudeau's ideas are worthy of a closer scrutiny.

Most of the articles he brought together in one volume in 1967,[2] Centennial year, date from the period when he was co-director, with Gérard Pelletier (now "Honourable" himself, in Ottawa), of an antiestablishment review, *Cité libre* (1950-1965). The Prime Minister of today, far from repudiating his rebel writings, reedited and published them after he had gone over to Ottawa and become the Minister of Justice. In his preface to the book, the cabinet minister Pelletier heaps up the praises he felt he should offer to the leader of his party: "I have no hesitation in saying that I consider Pierre Trudeau's work to be the most serious effort to formulate a political theory for Quebec and Canada that has been attempted in the past twenty-five years."[3]

The Prime Minister of Canada belongs to the long line of English liberals of the second half of the nineteenth century. He has all their reasoning ability, all their resourcefulness in argumentation. He is most fond of quoting Lord Acton. Familiar with the French writers as well, he is far from forgetting that Montesquieu praised

English parliamentary government and de Tocqueville the American democracy. "In view of the fact that it was the Canadian constitution that united the qualities of these two systems for the first time in history, it is rather paradoxical that French-Canadian 'thinkers' should have such difficulty in perceiving its merits."[4] In the very preface of his collection of articles, he shows the cloven hoof; this "thinkers" in quotation marks speaks volumes on his opinion of those who do not think like himself; unless of course the very fact of being French-Canadian irremediably disqualifies a person from taking the title of thinker; thinking would thus be another "occupation" reserved for other ethnic groups. But let's stop this quibbling and get back to the political system.

Because Trudeau sees enormous merit in the Canadian political system, Quebeckers should be happy with it, regardless of what is put in this empty framework, or what group controls the system. "The theory of checks and balances . . . has always had my full support. It translates into practical terms the concept of equilibrium that is inseparable from freedom in the realm of ideas."[5] These ideas of checks and balances and equilibrium are of fundamental importance for the Prime Minister. He is right to emphasize them, because they are the best theoretical guarantees of the status quo. Thus, given that Canadian Confederation has lasted for a century, the people of Quebec should not try to leave it, even if this regime appears unfavourable to them, because they would destroy that fine system of checks and balances and equilibrium which has worked so well for the English Canadians. The system's the important thing — it must be saved. Trudeau is so convinced of the virtues of the system that he sacrifices himself to it. "As I have explained, it was because of the federal government's weakness that I allowed myself to be catapulted into it."[6]

Opting for the system which incarnates the theory of checks and balances and equilibrium, he has no use for social and human realities. His utterances are so spare, so abstract that his system is perfectly suited to a nonexistent country. He is the Prime Minister of an intellectual viewpoint which is opposed with all its reason to any national sentiment. His great principle of opposition to the nation — a concrete reality, history in the flesh — is the State, a State become a kind of abstract universal, bereft of all humanity, which crowns the neutrality and imper- sonality of merchandise and money. The abstract uni- versality of the State, like that of money, masks the fact that dominant ethnic groups and social classes have the privilege of subjugating and oppressing less fortunate social classes and nations. We have shown, in the preceding chapter, what one hundred years of these principles have achieved in practise.

Trudeau's intentions, like those of his master Lord Acton, theoretician of checks and balances, are good. He does not want social classes or nations to be ruled and exploited in the name of some irrational principle like class struggle or national sentiment; he wants them to obey the voice of reason. What could be more praiseworthy? In his words, "The rise of reason in politics is an advance of law; for is not law an attempt to regulate the conduct of men in society rationally rather than emotionally?"[7] Who makes the law? To protect whose interests? Who is boss in this national State, the millionaires or the workers, the English Canadians or the French Canadians? Which culture pre- vails? Whoever asks himself these questions is labelled as an old-fashioned, backward nationalist. "If reason be the governing virtue of federalism, it would seem that Canada got off to a good start."[8] As Paul Chamberland puts it: "The *cultural genocide* which threatens Quebec society is deliberately forgotten. The practical need for a collective will to live, which conditions every aspect of social activity, is misrepresented as a backward particularism, all to justify the existence of Canada, a situation which in fact denies collective justice and liberty to the French-Canadian minority. The Trudeaus are no doubt preoccupied with 'reevaluating ... the universal attributes of man' — English-Canadian man, that is."[9]

The Prime Minister's concept of the State is not new. Behind all the rationalizations and the claims to justice, we find the idea of the nineteenth-century bourgeois State, well-known to every political scientist. "Insofar as the mechanisms of class oppression have become fully realized in the universal structure of economic relations, the State can limit its repressive function to 'guaranteeing the established order.' Henceforth, it can 'separate itself' from society and exist not only as a special machine for repression but . . . elevate itself to the rank of legality and right." The capitalist system "permits and presupposes the liberation of the individual from his particular limitations, from the natural determinations of his family and his social group." Where one ethnic group dominates another, the inferior parties must be freed from their national limitations. The universality so prized by Trudeau is the old abstract universality of the bourgeois State, not only because it erects itself upon an unchanged social reality, a reality which contradicts and negates it, but because it constitutes the necessary presuppostion and the guarantee of that social order. "This is why the State is not a mere illusion, an ideological mystification, but a concrete and organic element in the social and economic system of capitalism."[10]

A century of Confederation shows that the State has mystified only the colonized people. The colonial masters have received the dividends of this abstract universalism in staggering quantities of hard cash. What about the proletariat of the dominated nation? Trudeau replies that "the function of the State is to guarantee the establishment and maintenance of the kind of legal system in which the citizens can realize themselves to the full." Self-realization in a capitalist State means becoming the best possible consumer, without the hindrances of family and nation. The Prime Minister of Canada seems indifferent to the fact that in his State, ruled by law, order, rationality, equilibrium and checks and balances, there exist social classes, ethnic groups and nations which suffer injustice.

To be fair, we should note that some years ago Trudeau wrote: "Democracy cannot work in a country where a large number of citizens are condemned to the perpetual status of an oppressed people, whether that oppression take on an economic character or some other form." I would not do Mr. Trudeau the disservice of thinking that he believes, because he is head of the Canadian government, that he can change this state of perpetual domination by waving some magic wand. Let him read the analyses of his own economists; he will realize that he is dealing with a situation centuries old; it cannot be obliterated by clever turns of phrase or eccentric repartee.

But let's return to serious persons, to empire-builders, to Lord Acton, for example, who seems to have inspired Trudeau's antinationalist obsessions. In speaking of the nation, Lord Acton said: "Its course . . . will be marked with material as well as moral ruin, in order that a new invention may prevail over the works of God and the interests of mankind."[11] Trudeau adds: "Perhaps this new invention is functionalism, which will perhaps emerge as clearly inseparable from any viable concept of federalism."

It is interesting to note that the nation, a social reality, is far from having disappeared. Whether we like it or not, the national principle, as Henri Lefebvre remarks, has shaped the last century together with the principle of social class. More artificial realities like the British Empire or even the Commonwealth have had their day, while these two principles, to which men spontaneously adhere, have grown stronger in the last few years.

It is to say the least bizarre that Trudeau should want to replace nationality with functionalism. In seeing it as an "invention" which can substitute for the nation, he is confusing different orders of reality. Functionalism is not a human group and cannot replace nationality or the nation. If Fairchild's *Dictionary of Sociology* is right in saying that "The true nation is probably the most stable and coherent large-scale human group yet produced by social evolution,"[12] it is doubtful that the nation can ever be replaced by a principle of analysis, a theory, a sociology or an ideology — such as functionalism. Some people, in fact, see functionalism as nothing but a principle of analysis for the study of socioeconomic realities; others look upon it as a sociological theory; for some, perhaps for most people, functionalism is also an ideology. Many American functionalists, who hold that the function of every institution is to preserve the unity of society as a whole, favour the status quo and the equilibrium that results from it. Any attempt to change society, to put an end to the domination of one group by another, is for them dysfunctional, because such an attempt threatens the equilibrium of society, which ought to be preserved. Functionalism, for many sociologists, is a "guarantee of the established order." Because they are above all interested in the *functioning* of society, they are not concerned with knowing in favour of what group, of what class, of what nationality society has established its equilibrium and its checks and balances. In this view, applied functionalism must cure the deviationists who seek to disturb the balance of existing forces. As soon as Trudeau feels that the Canadian equilibrium is menaced, as soon as he realizes that the mood of Quebec has changed, he goes over to Ottawa: ". . . it was because of the federal government's weakness that I allowed myself to be catapulted into it." As ideology, functionalism is just this: one must not destroy an equilibrium created by a series of checks and balances.

Nevertheless, Trudeau's candid avowal — concerning an "invention" which would replace the nation — shows a certain doctrinal and political coherence. Functionalism, as a theory and as an ideology, appears as the crowning glory of the abstract universalism of the bourgeois State, likewise founded on the concept of equilibrium. It is concerned not with the content of human relationships, not with phenomena of change, but with the stability of relations established between social classes and between nations. It is a formalism with an undoubted appeal for constitutionalists like Trudeau. Functionalism, which dates from the late nineteenth and early twentieth centuries, is a quasi-scientific ideology which is at the antipodes in relation to class struggle, decolonization and all the liberation movements which are shaking our planet today and which aim at destroying the balance of power established by the middle classes and by the various imperialisms. This doctrine has been associated, historically, with a certain form of bourgeois State and with its activities of repression and domination. "We feel ourselves to be at the very end of our time, and suddenly we realize that History has entered a new phase without our knowing it" (Roger Vaillant, *The Balance Between Horse and Rabbit* [*L'equilibre entre le cheval et le lièvre*]).

Trudeau, an antinationalist, a functionalist and a statist, quite naturally wanted to preserve the balance of Canadian Confederation, a balance he saw threatened by Quebec. This was in 1967, before the revelations of the Royal Commission of Enquiry concerning the Quebec menace. Will he revise his stand and come back to Quebec? Up to now the only comment he has made about the revelations in *La Presse* is to the effect that the Canadian government will prosecute the people who filched these documents. Once Trudeau established the leading themes of his philosophy — State, checks and balances, equilibrium, reason, functionalism — what use did he make of them? In simple terms, he holds that Quebec is one of the ten provinces of Canada; the equilibrium is established on the basis of nine to one. Since Ottawa is in fact the "national" capital of Canada's English-speaking people, one might think Quebec City could be the national capital of the French-speaking people. This, however, would be an unhealthy balance. In Trudeau's words, "From a constitutional point of view, the Quebec Legislature has no authority to speak on behalf of 'French Canada.' French Canada includes 850,000

Canadians whose mother tongue is French, who live outside Quebec, and over whom the Legislature has no jurisdiction."[13] This is a main point in every one of Trudeau's arguments for equilibrium, and will carry some weight until all of these 850,000 individuals have been assimilated. As the present rate of assimilation is steadily increasing, the constitutional argument may soon be obsolete. For the time being, these people are hostages who allow Ottawa to maintain, legally and constitutionally, the system of checks and balances and equilibrium which has been established for the last century.

Here is how things have gone for French-speaking North Americans since the beginning of Confederation. In 1867, Quebec was one of the *four* Canadian provinces, along with Ontario, New Brunswick and Nova Scotia. A hundred years later, Quebec is one of ten provinces. Prince Edward Island, with a population of 100,000, has the same status as Quebec in this regard. In 1867, Quebec occupied five-ninths of the Canadian territory; today it has only one-seventh of the total area. In Quebec, the proportion of French-speaking people has increased to 83.3 per cent of the total population in 1961. Outside of Quebec, the French Canadians have steadily lost ground; in 1931, French-speaking people living outside of Quebec represented 19 per cent of all French-speakers in Canada, but in 1961 this group amounted to only 16 per cent. The number of Canadians of French origin who become anglicized, i.e., who declare to census-takers that English is their mother tongue, has steadily increased: 3.5 per cent in 1921, 7.9 per cent in 1951, and 10 per cent in 1961. Professor Henripin predicts that by the most favourable hypothesis the French-Canadian element will be no more than 20 per cent of Canada's total population within 40 years; a more pessimistic estimate puts the figure at 17 per cent, which would be about half the proportion that French Canadians represented in 1867. In Newfoundland, "We find a population of French origin which has been 80 per cent anglicized."[14] In Prince Edward Island, "more than half the people of French origin no longer know any language but English, and the rest are apparently becoming anglicized at a rapid rate. In 1941, for example, the number of Canadians of French origin declaring English as their native language was only 29.1 per cent; in 1961 this same category had increased to 55.2 per cent." In Nova Scotia, "of 100 Canadians of French descent only 47 still know French, while in 1931 there were 71 . . ." In New Brunswick, where the French-speaking people are more grouped together, the losses have not been as heavy; close to 90 per cent of French Canadians there know French and nearly 88 per cent still declare French to be their native language. In Ontario, anglicization has proceeded more rapidly than in New Brunswick. "In Ontario, the French-speaking minority knows more English than French (85 per cent as against 66 per cent); 61.4 per cent of this group declare English to be their mother tongue." The four western provinces of Canada are a disaster area. In the category of people of French descent, those who tell census-takers that they know only English amount to 30 per cent in Manitoba, 40 per cent in Saskatchewan, 48.8 per cent in Alberta, and 60 per cent in British Columbia. When the Prime Minister speaks of the 850,000 French Canadians living in Canada outside of Quebec, we must ask just what this figure represents. Ottawa is using pure blackmail in claiming the right to rule French Canada on the grounds that there are French Canadians living outside of Quebec. A good part of Trudeau's arguments in favour of federalism are based on this group outside of Quebec; there is not much left of them when we realize how rapidly Confederation is anglicizing Canadians of French origin. In some cases, anglicization is as rapid as in New Orleans, where the country is officially monolingual. Outside of Quebec, nearly half a million French-speaking people have already been assimilated. When the people of Quebec react against the slow genocide, Trudeau calls them racists and Nazis.

Trudeau has said: "As a matter of fact, I might be

prepared to argue that some day, if and when *inter alia* the political maturity of all Canadians had reached a very high level, a more centralized state would be acceptable for Canada."[15] This dream will no doubt become possible when all the French Canadians have been anglicized.

How does Trudeau presently react to the growing separatist forces in Quebec? He heaps sarcasm on the separatists; lets them be bludgeoned by the police (June 24, 1968); makes every effort to prevent their involvement in the international French-speaking community; ridicules the French (e.g., his remark "Long live the free franc" during the monetary crisis of May 1968). Moreover, this smiter of nationalism, of all nationalisms ("The nation-state idea is absurd in principle and retrograde in practice . . ."), wrote in 1964: "One way of offsetting the appeal of separatism is by investing tremendous amounts of time, energy, and money in nationalism, at the *federal level*. A national image must be created that will have such an appeal as to make any image of a separatist group unattractive. Resources must be diverted into such things as national flags, anthems, education, arts councils, broadcasting corporations, film boards . . . In short, the whole of the citizenry must be made to feel that it is only within the framework of the federal state that their language, culture, institutions, sacred traditions, and standard of living can be protected from external attack and internal strife. It is, of course, obvious that a national consensus will be developed in this way only if the nationalism is emotionally acceptable to all important groups within the nation."[16] Some intellectual loop the loop! Here we are back with the old dreams of Durham, of the Fathers of Confederation: make a state into a nation, create a nationalism. A hundred and thirty-one years after 1840, the bad penny has turned up again. No matter, Ottawa is prepared to carry on with the comedy by spending "tremendous amounts of money," as Trudeau puts it. It's always the same old cultural genocide in a new disguise. André d'Allemagne is right in saying: "Confederation is a genocide without end."[17]

On the whole, Trudeau's arguments against independence for Quebec, apart from his theoretical arguments against the nation State and in favour of the abstract State, can be reduced to three: first of all, the complaints Quebeckers make against Confederation ought to be made against their own elites and their own politicians, because they are the ones who have not adopted progressive ways; secondly, a politically independent Quebec is not viable economically; thirdly, there are French-speaking people outside of Quebec who would be abandoned if Quebec left Confederation. We shall run across these arguments again in the following chapters.

Chapter 8
Quebec or French Canada?

In 1968, in his year-end speech, General de Gaulle expressed the hope that the French people of Canada would obtain a free hand in the management of their national life. The journalists at once remarked that the General had been more insistent on this point than the previous year. When asked about this statement, the Prime Minister of Canada, Mr. Trudeau, was said to have agreed with the General. How was this possible? "The General was speaking of French Canada," Trudeau is said to have replied, "not of Quebec." The essence of the Quebec problem lies, in fact, in this distinction.

To speak of French Canada (or of the French people of Canada) is to speak of Canadians who speak French and who live in all parts of Canada. The problem is therefore one of bilingualism or at the most of biculturalism, and the solution is to be reached through the agency of the central government, the Canadian State. Federalists are happy to grant the name of French Canada to the totality of French-speaking people scattered throughout the Canadian territory. Ottawa could, at the outside, even tolerate that this same population be called the French-Canadian nation, because so defined the word "nation" refers only to characteristics of language and culture; moreover, Ottawa remains the government of these two "nations" because we are speaking of a population distributed over the entire territory of Canada. The French-speaking people thus remain the traditional minority of about 28 per cent, defending their minority rights while experiencing a progressive anglicization. All is safe and sound. No attack has been made on the political and economic power structure, nor on the important sectors of government and administration which continue to be controlled by the central government in Ottawa, the capital of the two "nations." Here is the most perfect status quo, the very thesis of Mr. Trudeau. For the federalists, Quebec is *one* province out of *ten*; it can make no claims to represent the French-Canadian nation because there are still French-speaking people living in the other nine provinces.

In the 1960's a great change occurred, revolutionizing the situation. In Quebec, people began to make a distinction between Quebec and French Canada. On the one hand, there is a population of French-speaking people distributed throughout Canada. This population has, in varying degrees, a common heritage of language, religion, tradition and custom. This cultural element represents about 28 per cent of Canada's total population. Federal government statistics show that outside of Quebec this population is becoming anglicized at various rates of speed; in British Columbia 60 per cent of this group have been assimilated. For Canada as a whole, it's a lost cause sooner or later; the steamroller of English-speaking North American culture will soon leave nothing but a few remnants of this language and culture.

On the other hand, there is a vast land three times larger than France where the French-speaking people are a great majority, namely Quebec. Since 1867, this territory has had a government and an administration with limited constitutional powers, but still perhaps capable of exercising enough leverage to safeguard most of what we call French Canadian culture. On the evidence, to do this requires a reevaluation of the Quebec State, the only collective instrument that the French Canadians possess. As we have already seen, even in this State of Quebec the French-speaking people own only a small share of the economy, of the industry and commerce. All they have is a mini-state, a territory, a culture and the desire to live together and to develop themselves. Under the pressure of public opinion, Quebec provincial governments have timidly endeavoured, since 1960, to affirm this State and to control, as far as possible, those economic and political decisions which affect the life of their people. They have adopted measures to strengthen the role of the State in economic life. They soon realized, however, that the most important powers required by a modern industrial state were held by the national government of the other nine provinces, in all of which the English-speaking people were in the majority. Quebec public opinion showed a surprising degree of unanimity in favouring more power for the Quebec State, and a significant part of the population now demanded full political powers for Quebec. It is here that the Quebec question arises. We are no longer dealing with French Canada, with bilingualism and biculturalism, but with the powers of the State of Quebec and with the collective life of the people of Quebec. It is not a matter of nationalism, racism or prejudice towards anyone; it is simply a question of life or death for a nation of six million people. The fate of Canada's French-speaking people will be decided in Quebec itself. In Newfoundland, in British Columbia, French Canada's culture is finished — in Ottawa too. A century of Confederation has proved that.

Why is Ottawa so hostile? Why do all the English-speaking people, all the "businessmen" deploy all their money and their propaganda against the idea of independence for Quebec, or even of a rearrangement of powers between Quebec and Ottawa? Quite simply, they realize that after a hundred years of Confederation they are on the point of winning. The French-speaking people of North America are now playing their last trump card, in Quebec and especially in Montreal. In industry and commerce, the French-speaking people of Montreal have been dominated by the English Canadians, even in their own city. In the last few years they have become more and more aware of a new danger: French may become the language of a minority in Quebec itself sooner or later. The St. Léonard affair has recently brought this situation to the attention of the public.

In the Canadian Confederation, French-speaking people are in the minority everywhere. Even the Quebeckers feel this way. One province in ten doesn't amount to much. The English-speaking minority of Montreal considers itself a majority because it belongs to Canada's dominant group. The British North America Act, the legal foundation of Canada's existence, grants Protestant public schools to the English-speaking people of Quebec. Concentrated for the most part in Montreal, this 10 per cent minority lives in the best part of town (Westmount, Mount Royal, Hampstead), controls economic and industrial life, is paid the highest salaries and has its own schools. In the province of Quebec, this 10 per cent minority has three universities (McGill, Sir George Williams, Bishop's), as many as the French-speaking group. The English Canadians use the schools so graciously provided by the provincial government to anglicize the immigrants who settle in Quebec. "In Montreal, which receives 85 per cent of the immigration to Quebec, 90 per cent of the children of these immigrants go to English schools. Considering the rate at which immigrants are being assimilated to the English-speaking minority, and the decline in the birthrate of French-speaking Quebeckers (down 23 per cent from 1964 to 1968), French-Canadian social critics are led to the conclusion that their people will soon be a minority in their own province; according to them, Montreal is sure to become an English-speaking city in ten years; Quebec itself has a reprieve of twenty years. This fear of becoming a minority was behind what happened in St. Léonard. An invitation to a public demonstration even asked the question: "Are French Canadians going to disappear?"[1]

St. Léonard is a town in the suburbs of Montreal. The local school board wanted to force the Italian immigrants there to send their children to the French schools. The English Canadians protested vigorously and thousands of them marched on Ottawa to protest the measures taken by the town council of St. Léonard. People in Quebec and the rest of Canada were entranced by the affair, which revealed the enfeebled position of French Canadians even in their own country, Quebec. As in all cases of judicial murder, everything was done under the cover of the law; in a liberal democracy we act in the name of the freedom of individuals to choose the language and the school in which their children shall be educated. A separatist leader has written in this connection: "Thus the system of public schools in English not only keeps the Anglo-Saxons on the fringes of Quebec society, but also attracts all the other ethnic minorities to these fringes; it even appeals to a growing number of French-speaking people, because of the economic ascendancy of this Anglo-Saxon minority within Quebec, a minority which is supported by a vast majority outside the province."[2]

In June 1968, in an open letter to *La Presse,* one of its readers said: "The present government [*Union Nationale*], or a Liberal government for that matter, will never be willing to face up to our linguistic situation, to recognize that we, the French-speaking Quebeckers, are losing ground in terms of population . . . our two leading parties, the *Union Nationale* and the Liberals, like their opposite numbers in federal politics, are tied to the financial interests which control our destiny. When money talks, it speaks English . . ." When the St. Léonard controversy broke out, Quebeckers suddenly realized that a community was being destroyed in the name of Trudeau's brand of liberal democracy. The journalist Jean-Marc Léger was thus moved to write that it is wrong "to hold that the rights of the individual can be exercised absolutely, without being limited by the rights of the collectivity, of the national community, whose basic right is to exist and to ensure its continued existence."[3] The trouble is that Ottawa only recognizes the political community of Canada; it acknowledges that there are French-speaking individuals scattered throughout the State of Canada, and that these people have a right, as individuals, to attend French schools (when there are any).

Most of the French Canadians involved in the St. Léonard dispute have suggested two remedies to the situation: that French become the sole language of instruction in the Quebec public school system, and that Quebec establish an immigration policy with all possible speed. The St. Léonard movement was not initiated by political parties or by ideologists, but by "fathers and mothers who had never demonstrated in their lives."[4] In the same vein, Jean-Marc Léger-wrote: "We must have in Quebec, especially in the Montreal area, ten, twenty, fifty St. Léonards. We must coordinate all these efforts in a vast movement to safeguard our nation; we must force the government to protect and foster French schools, to adopt an education policy which will effectively bring about the integration of the immigrants into our community . . ."[5]

We wonder if such a course of action could lead to the desired results as long as the State of Quebec continues to be a minority within Confederation, a regional government with limited control over its economic and political life. In the last hundred years, so many would-be national saviours have run smack into a brick wall: the power of financial and political oligarchies. It is no longer the culture which must be saved, but the very existence of the community.

The English-Canadian Reaction

St. Léonard wanted to prevent the anglicization of its immigrants, and of its French-speaking people as well. This affair did not leave English Canadians unmoved. The St. Léonard controversy echoed in every quarter, in every part of Canada; it involved matters so relevant to the survival of Quebec that it figured in some of the predictions regarding the province's economic growth in the coming year, 1969. The St. Léonard issue concerned only immigrants whose native language was not English. The English-speaking people of Quebec were not directly menaced by it; still, they were wholeheartedly opposed to the St. Léonard school board, which wanted its immigrant children to receive their schooling in the language of the country. Which country, Quebec or Canada? Given the present state of things, the immigrants and the English-speaking people, of Quebec and elsewhere, are right to want a continuation of the old school policies. If the immigrants who land in Quebec feel they have settled in Canada, for the most part a country of English language and culture, they are clearly justified in wanting to become anglicized as quickly as possible; then, too, the United States speaks English. The English Canadians of Montreal live in an English-speaking country, Canada; why should they not woo the immigrants who have settled in a part of this Canada? They control industry, finance and commerce; do they not need workers who can understand their language? Nothing could be more normal. The French-speaking people may have to bear the cost of all these normal arrangements; that is no concern of the English-speaking Canadians and the immigrants. It is a concern, however, of the French Canadians. Let us admit that up to now they have not welcomed immigrants with open arms. They are a minority in Confederation, and are dominated and exploited in their own country, Quebec. Traditionally, they have tended to confine themselves to their own ethnic group, and to act very standoffish towards immigrants. In the past, moreover, the immigrants were English-speaking people who swelled the dominant majority; how could the French Canadians be delighted at their arrival in Quebec? A nation of itinerant labourers, Quebeckers suffered the highest rate of unemployment in Canada; any immigrant was a rival for the few available jobs. It was entirely to the immigrants' advantage to learn the language of the rich; moreover, the *"joual"*[6] employed by some French-speaking people perhaps seemed a difficult language to master.

Whatever their attitude in the past, a growing number of Quebeckers seem to be aware of the infernal process which is turning them into a minority in their own country; they have decided to stop it. It is doubtful, however, that they can succeed unless they take action on the political and economic level; such action is clearly impossible within the present confines of Confederation, where all the dice are loaded against the French Canadians.

A student of the Social Sciences Faculty of the University of Montreal, Anne Légaré, has attempted to find out what the English Canadians themselves consider to be at the root of the St. Léonard crisis; the results of her enquiry are very instructive, and I quote from them extensively below. Two English-Canadian organizations, the Montreal Board of Trade and the Presbytery of Montreal of the Presbyterian Church in Canada, have expressed their opinion of the St. Léonard crisis. Anne Légaré has analysed their press statements and has interviewed the moderator of the Presbyterian Church.

The Board of Trade has a membership of 3200 business organizations represented by about 7000 delegates. The Presbytery is the council for 45 churches, and each church chooses two delegates to the council from the group of businessmen who run the affairs of the local church congregation. We are thus dealing with two important institutions of the English-speaking minority in Montreal, where the connection between the "Protestant ethic" and the spirit of capitalism is obvious.

Beyond the linguistic issue, these two associations think that what is really at stake in the St. Léonard crisis is the value systems conveyed by the two languages. For them, English is the language of business, and the English-speaking people have constructed around this language a system of education which is adapted to the world of business. The Presbyterian moderator offered this advice to the French-speaking people: "Change your system of education, make it more pragmatic; classical education is not good for business." The Board of Trade put it this way: "The English, Protestant system of education aims at preparing a man for business." The Presbytery was of the opinion that "the French-Canadian system of education has not produced businessmen; the English-Canadian system has done so because it is more pragmatic." Although the moderator of the Presbyterian

Church believed that "Quebec nationalism, like the hippie phenomenon, is a revolt against the materialism of our society," he still concluded that Quebec is a menace to business. He also regarded the survival of the French-Canadian people in North America as the sign of a cultural resistance to the overwhelming presence of the dominant culture; he felt that the desire of some Quebec nationalists to integrate the Anglo-Saxons to French-Canadian culture was an attack on the only group in Quebec capable of survival and progress. Quebec's ideological resistance was, in his view, a total menace to the economic growth and prosperity of the English-speaking group.

The remedy proposed was simple. Both the Board and the Presbytery felt that the ideological difference between these two groups must be abolished by a school system adapted to "the prevailing orientation of our country [i.e., Canada] and of the continent." For Quebec, a rapprochement on these terms means falling into step with everyone else. The French-speaking people are expected to adopt the ideology and values of the Anglo-Protestants. The Presbyterian moderator was explicit on this point: "Everywhere in the world, but especially in North America, including Quebec, the English language is now an absolute necessity from the economic point of view . . . the English-speaking people of Quebec have no alternative but to force more and more people to accept the English system and to learn English."

One hundred and thirty years after the Durham Report, the verdict is the same: assimilate the French Canadians. The merely partial success of such efforts in all these years should not be unduly reassuring to Quebeckers. Fernand Dumont explains: "Our collective ignorance will save us for a while yet. Even when they left the country to come to the city, our proletarian contingents have been cooped up in districts and in occupations where they have clung to speech and behaviour patterns which are more or less bastardized but still distinctive. Let us not speak too unkindly of *joual. Joual* has been, and still is, our most faithful companion and the most incontrovertible proof of our survival."[7]

In other words, Quebec is continuing a struggle whose roots go deep into the past. Will the French Canadians be able to steer the course that will keep them from foundering? Some Quebeckers, who live outside Montreal in almost exclusively French-speaking areas, sometimes dream of abandoning the city to the "foreigners" in order to perpetuate the Quebec nation in the rest of the province, in a state of pure and unalloyed Frenchness. To dream thus is to sanctify the notion that Quebec could become a folklore reserve for North American tourists, a kind of monster Louisiana where people would flock from all over to celebrate the Mardi Gras and Mid-Lent. We must realize that Montreal is Quebec's last trump card. If the people's awareness of their servile and inferior condition continues to grow, all is not lost. If we retreat to hideaways in the country, we will have committed suicide in no time.

Chapter 9
Towards a Free Quebec?

Given Quebec's history of struggle and the difficulties that assail it on every hand, might we not wonder if, after all, the federalists are not right? In our present-day world, everything is tending towards unity and uniformity; for technology, for economic activity, there are no frontiers. Why then are we so persistent in our desire to save this French-speaking island, this Quebec nation in the midst of 200 million English-speaking people, the richest and most powerful people in the world? Why not resign ourselves to making Quebec a giant tourist attraction, on a truly North American scale? Quebeckers, instead of wrestling with an insoluble problem, would have only to pursue the course that has been so clearly mapped out for them. The French-speaking people who live outside Quebec are already well on the way to linguistic and cultural assimilation; Quebec itself is threatened by anglicization in its metropolitan and industrial area. If Quebeckers were only more willing to abandon all belief in themselves, the federalist program could be carried out without much difficulty. Everywhere we hear the refrain that Canada cannot be saved without this sacrifice. Have we sufficiently asked ourselves, "What is Canada?" When all is said and done, this collection of provinces is a group of North American territories which by language, history and customs have much in common with other parts of the continent. These provinces resemble each other less than each of them resembles the American state it borders on. They are bound together by a vague nostalgia for the British Crown; by a government which maintains a railway and an airline to promote trade among them; and by television and radio networks which broadcast American programs, interspersed with commercials sponsored by the Canadian subsidiaries of American companies. What do these provinces have above all in common? A "French problem!" We might briefly define Canada as a collection of North American territories whose major problem is not the Black problem. In the last few years, people have said time and again that without the "French problem" Canada would break up; the damning portrait I have sketched above is plausible enough.

It is sometimes argued that Quebec should remain in Confederation for the sake of economic efficiency. Why then make a detour via Newfoundland or Alberta when New York and Boston are much closer? Fernand Dumont writes: "Some have said that all nations must bow to the requirements of modern technological society, and yet have maintained that we must have a Canada in opposition to the United States. This seems to me a flagrant contradiction and the worst sort of regionalist timidity."

On the other hand, the Prime Minister of Canada, Mr. Trudeau, invites Quebeckers to join Canada in founding a nation, in producing the blossoms of a federal nationalism. The people of Quebec are already a nation and have already produced a "nationalism." Trudeau's demands are unreasonable; should the French Canadians destroy themselves in order to build, from scratch, a nation which up to now has been nothing but a creature of reason? There is also a major paradox in the thinking of the federalists: they have nothing but contempt and disdain for Quebec nationalism and yet, somewhat like the colonizers of Africa, they would ruin a historically rooted society in order to create a political agglomeration whose only ties are commercial interests.

The Quebec question still awaits an answer. Even those who admit the existence of a Quebec nation have only added another string to their bow. They say that a nation as poor and backward as Quebec would be better off as part of a vast political complex like Canada or the United States. One may well wonder, in all good faith, if there is a future for Quebec man. Does this species of humanity have any chance of survival in the world of the future, or of the present for that matter? The wolf ate Mr. Séguin's goat in the morning, though she had fought it off all night.[1] It would not be dishonourable for the people of Quebec, after two centuries of struggle, to admit that they are no longer big enough to last as an independent nation in a world of giant states. What would happen in such a case? The immediate prospects for Quebec are not very brilliant. In the census of 1961, 61.88 per cent of the Quebec population spoke only French, and French was the sole language of 77 per cent of the people living outside Montreal. Remember that even the assimilated French Canadian is not as successful as the English Canadian. Several decades would be needed to complete the anglicization of Quebeckers, and several more decades before their French-Canadian origin was completely forgotten. A man does not shed his culture and his nation as he pleases, as the American Indians know only too well. After centuries of attempted assimilation to English-speaking or French-speaking communities, they are still Indians. The simple annexation of Quebec to the United States or to Canada does not seem to be the miraculous solution that some people have seen in it.

The compromise solution, the federalist solution, has already been tried for the last hundred years, and we have revealed the results of this social experiment in the preceding chapters. It's a slow death, a program of mongrelization, *franglais*[2] sanctified as an institution. A carpetbagger's paradise! And how costly, how frustrating, how exhausting! The English Canadians and the Americans swing big deals and throw up industrial plants. We French Canadians fight for bilingual postage stamps; we invent a hundred subterfuges to attend a convention of French-speaking nations in the Congo; we translate the latest speeches of Robert Stanfield and Paul Martin; we are continually called upon to reply to the question: "What does Quebec want?" We provide the Americans with weapons to murder people in Vietnam, and we help to build mighty systems of defense against the Russians.

These systems are obsolete as soon as they are finished, and we start all over again. We pay the salaries of all the federal agents who come to Quebec to govern us in English, and yet the federalists accuse us of having a siege mentality. Federal radio and television carry on a perpetual campaign in favour of a creature of reason, Canada. Some techniques are more annoying than others. When pictures of Nancy Green skiing are shown on the television screen, the commentator feels he has to mention the words "Canada" and "Canadian" ten times. Still, we don't mind too much; we see Nancy Green, who is pretty, and an expanse of virgin snow. When, however, a Montrealer is leaving for work and turns on the radio to find out if it will rain that day, he first has to listen to weather forecasts for a whole series of cities he doesn't know and doesn't give a damn about; he has to make a trip around the world to get to Montreal. This is infuriating. The gimmick is so obvious; at all costs, the Quebecker must have this day his daily Canada . . . sunny skies in Prince Rupert, Edmonton, Fredericton . . . rain in Toronto, Kapuskasing, Victoria, Saskatoon . . . Exasperated, our Montrealer leaves his home without learning that a high-pressure disturbance is sweeping down on him at a terrible speed.

Mr. Trudeau would be among the first to reply that these are truly minor disadvantages, considering that Canada has one of the highest standards of living in the world. This is true enough, but how much do Quebeckers share in it, or even French Canadians in the rest of Canada? In every region of this affluent land, they are the least prosperous, the most unemployed, and yet they become more anglicized every day! In their own country, they are the lumpenproletariat! Federalists insist that Confederation is the good life, independence the blackest misery, but we wonder if the people of Quebec can sink any lower. They do not seem to have much to lose.

We have been told for some time that all this will be changed in short order. A great team is in power in Ottawa that will establish bilingualism from one ocean to the other. Perhaps the best way to prevent English Canadians from prospering is to make them bilingual and bicultural; Ottawa's statistics prove, in fact, that bilingual people are less successful than those who know only English. Imagine the English Canadians falling into this trap! This team, like its leader, believes that "it is better to free man by technical progress; he can concern himself with culture afterwards." For such men to recommend the bilingual and bicultural solution seems somewhat paradoxical, for they will thereby be concerning themselves primarily with two languages and two cultures. In any case, there are more and more Quebeckers who intend to relax and become monolingual and monocultural like everybody else.

Quebeckers Are Condemned to Remain a People

However we envisage the problem, we realize that there is only one solution for Quebec: to keep on living and struggling for its existence. The only question to be asked is whether the people of Quebec are condemned to be nothing but hewers of wood and drawers of water or, on a more advanced level, translators and members of Parliament. The great majority of Quebeckers, and even Quebec's traditional political parties, have rejected the status quo; even the Quebec Liberal party, probably the most pro-Ottawa party in Quebec, demands a revision of the constitution. At the other end of the political spectrum, the supporters of separatism appear to be getting more and more numerous. It thus seems reasonable to predict that sooner or later Quebec will obtain a greater autonomy within Confederation, if not complete independence. Nobody can tell which alternative will prevail in the near future.

At a time when Quebec is seeking political autonomy or even independence, what light can we throw on its future? Given Quebec's history, with the peculiar conditions of domination and colonization that have characterized it and to a large extent still do, we have a right to wonder what use it would make of its greater autonomy or independence. In other words, we may ask not only what the future of Quebec man will be, but what the future of Quebec society will be. There does not seem to be a historical precedent or a sociological model which would help us predict the evolution of the Quebec community. In many respects, its case is unique. We may observe once more that the nature of the predictions will depend on the analysis first made of the Quebec problem. For the federalists who consider only the economic factor, viewed in the narrow perspective of economic growth, the future of Quebec is no great problem. They assume that the wealthy provinces and the big money-lenders can be persuaded to accept a policy of equalization which would reduce regional disparities. Given the overall strength of the Canadian economy, the federalists feel they can quickly supply an answer to our question. Their reply is as valid as any analysis which fails to consider historical, cultural or ideological factors; it is the resurrection of *homo economicus* out of the nineteenth century.

If, on the contrary, we try to take other aspects of the problem into account, our answers will be less simple but closer to reality. For a long time, the Americans believed that the problems of Latin America or of their own Blacks could be resolved by vague projects of economic equalization; today they realize that there is more, much more involved than a simple matter of distributing surplus monies.

The Doubtful Privilege of Underdevelopment

At the beginning of the Quiet Revolution, some of us believed that certain theories arrived at by biologists, anthropologists and political thinkers (Veblen and Trotsky are the most famous) were going to apply in their totality to Quebec.[3] Perhaps we are too close to the events to judge accurately, but we realize that though these theories may work automatically in biology, they do not operate as uniformly where human societies are concerned. It is not clear whether these generalizations are going to describe every aspect of Quebec society; should they not apply universally, it is not even possible to predict in which areas they are most likely to be valid.

Let us briefly describe our analysis of the problem at the start of the Quiet Revolution. We began by making almost the same kind of observation as has been recently made by Marshall McLuhan. For McLuhan, Quebec has just jumped two centuries, from the seventeenth to the twentieth, and the French Canadians have great difficulty getting along with the English Canadians who are still living in the nineteenth century, when Anglo-Saxon culture ruled the world. Our sociological observations were not quite McLuhan's paradoxes. It did seem to us, however, that Quebec was beginning to see itself as an advanced industrial society and to define itself in those terms, but the bulk of its population still had a largely traditional mentality, culture and outlook on the world. Even in Montreal and in the other cities of Quebec, people were still able to live much as they had always lived in their villages and parishes. Many of their institutions protected them from change: the extended family, the parish, the Catholic religion, the rich oral tradition. Compared to people in other parts of North America, the French Canadians had not been deeply affected by the sociocultural phenomena which accompany urbanization: individualization, impersonality, and the secularization and atomization of society.

The keenest minds in Quebec soon realized that although the conduct of their elites might partially explain their backwardness in many areas, the domination of Quebec's people by foreign groups was an important factor as well. In the Gaspé, for example, a whole region remained entirely dependent on entrepreneurs who were against sending the people to school, on the grounds that education would not make them into better fishermen. We find the same thing in university education. "For the academic year 1933-1934, the University of Montreal, by paring its budget to the absolute minimum, had reduced its expenses to $416,678 ... For the same year, McGill University had a budget of $2,577,932,"[4] i.e., six times the budget for a population six or seven times smaller than the French-speaking population of Montreal. Still, in the overall picture of underdevelopment, the Catholic Church and the Quebec government had much to answer for. At the moment, then, that the people of Quebec became conscious of what they were and began to want to control their own destiny, the great social phenomena of our time also made their appearance: decolonization, underdevelopment, confrontation. We observed a conjunction of these two series of phenomena, an interaction between them. Civilization was everywhere in crisis. In the early 1960's, we felt that Quebec, less tied to the old order of things than its North American neighbours, could more easily find solutions to the new problems confronting humanity. This was what we meant by the privilege of underdevelopment. We soon found ourselves faced with a very concrete dilemma: whether just to catch up with our neighbours, or to try to surpass them. The two main ideologies at war in Quebec have centred on this problem. Must we simply catch up, i.e., get in step with our neighbours by doing what they have already done long ago, or must we try, while we are catching up, to make ourselves more adapted to today's society, and to tomorrow's as well? The first solution is easier and less risky; the second requires much more creative imagination and, in the short term at least, would force us to take more chances.

A few years have passed since we made these analyses and asked these questions. In some fields, Quebec seems determined to surpass its neighbours; education is the best example. It has not persevered as much in the economic domain, and this does not seem wholly due to the fact that foreign interests control the country's economy. In the early 1960's Quebec did not have a unified system of education; having appointed a Royal Commission and accepted its recommendations, it was therefore able to establish a system of education which is one of the best adapted in the world to the work which confronts us all in the latter part of the twentieth century. It would have been totally ridiculous for Quebec to copy any existing system, even of a nation which had already succeeded; the tasks of today and tomorrow are not those of yesterday. Here is a situation where, from some points of view, it is an advantage to be underdeveloped.

In our efforts to catch up, how can we distinguish between the essential undertakings and those which lead to a dead end? The underdeveloped country may be racing to catch up with the nations ahead of it, but it does not have to take the same road to reach the same destination; it can take shortcuts. The front-runners have had to pay the cost of false starts that the laggards can avoid. A small nation with limited resources like Quebec can succeed only by making better use of its energy and its capital than bigger countries; it is less entitled to make mistakes. In periods of rapid change, underdevelopment can be an advantage, provided that the underdeveloped country does not have its undertakings controlled by foreigners who dominate and exploit it. For a backward people, there is nothing more tragic than to follow a country which has already gone off in some other direction. It has often been recognized that the French-speaking people of Quebec, by limiting themselves to programs for catching up, are leaving themselves forever behind the times. The colonial masters could hardly ask for more; they are glad to help their subjects to cling to such good habits.

For many years, a certain social arrangement in Quebec has suited the interests of English-Canadian and American exploiters; it is still completely satisfactory from their point of view. In this arrangement, the French-speaking people of Quebec devote themselves to certain undertakings, to certain industries and services which are no doubt essential, but which do not offer the best revenues or the most brilliant futures. Some Quebeckers have managed to obtain good jobs and some importance in the economic and industrial structures that the foreigners have established in Quebec; these people are doing everything in their power to preserve the status quo. The French-Canadian employee of these institutions is usually the most ardent supporter of Confederation and the foreign interests. We find the same phenomenon in the linguistic field; the bilingual intermediaries are energetically opposed to a French-only policy in Quebec, because they would thereby lose their jobs as parasitical go-betweens.

Catching Up and Surpassing

The notions of catching up and of surpassing are central to the two great ideologies which are presently wooing the people of Quebec. The ideology of catching up, which on the political level is above all federalist, recognizes that Quebec is behind the times in many areas. It tends to attribute this underdevelopment to the Quebeckers themselves, and greatly minimizes the consequences of the British conquest of 1760 and of the Anglo-Saxon control of Quebec's economy and industry which followed. This school of thought holds that Quebec has for too long indulged itself in the idea that it could create a society with a special mission in North America. This is in fact a denial of Quebec as a true nation, because a social group cannot be a nation unless it has a distinct program for communal existence. Renan said that a nation is the desire of many individuals to do great things together, and the English anthropologist Nadel defines a nation as the theory that its members have of it. One may debate the merits of this or that collective program or theory, but to deny that these things can be is, unquestionably, to deny the existence of nations. The federalists have a coherent platform, and all its planks point in the same direction. The day that Quebec entrusts Canada or the United States with the determination of its collective purpose, there will be no more nation of Quebec. This is in fact what is recommended by the ideology of catching up: Quebec should become a North American territory like the others and should abandon the idea that the people of Quebec can "do great things together." Contrary to what the most generous – or the least aware – federalists believe, a culture and a nation whose only distinctive trait was language would soon cease to be a culture and a nation. It would soon lose even its language; the half-million French Canadians anglicized by Confederation are the defunct proof of that.

The adherents of the doctrine of catching up have another favourite idea: each man must look out for himself in a humanity composed of individuals. They say to Quebeckers, "Why put yourself out for the community, why demand your national rights, why dream of a free Quebec when each of you can become rich and successful for himself?" Their enquiries prove that even those who follow their advice and assimilate are no more successful than the other French Canadians, because the fact of belonging, or of having belonged, to an ethnic group is in this case the determining factor in success.

The basic federalist idea seems to be that the people of Quebec should go through a complete phase of nineteenth-century liberal democracy; that they should thoroughly involve themselves in the sort of overcompetitive society that more and more people in industrialized countries have already begun to reject. Why should Quebeckers, at a time when they are becoming masters of their fate, adopt Lord Acton[5] as a patron saint? They don't have to give themselves an inferiority or guilt complex because they have not always practised English democracy, or because they do not practise it perfectly today. Everywhere in the world, people are searching for other forms of participation in social and political life. The people of Quebec must look elsewhere too, and invent –

why not? — new forms of democracy.

While undertaking the necessary task of catching up, Quebec must make every effort to develop an original type of society; such a society should take into account that Quebec is an integral part both of North America and of the international French-speaking community.

The ideology which looks beyond catching up appeared in the wake of the Quiet Revolution of 1960. Its leading concepts are participation, development and surpassing. It favours economic growth, of course — what collectivity can be indifferent to this imperative? The difference here is that economic growth is not the only imperative, nor the one that subordinates all other sociocultural imperatives, as in liberal democracy. Instead of making a detour into the bourgeois revolution, instead of trying to create a bourgeoisie to replace foreign economic agents, this theory finds it more realistic and less expensive to aim at a participatory democracy. History does not repeat itself. The conditions which have favoured the ascendency of a national bourgeoisie in other countries do not exist in Quebec. The only collective leverage available to the French-speaking people of this country is the Quebec State. It is this State which in the early stages can begin to rectify and redirect the Quebec economy, while at the same time encouraging functional groups to participate in the government. The old nationalism, reflected in the conservative ideology, took its model of society from the colonial master; its leaders merely wanted to replace the foreign capitalism which exploited the country by a native capitalism. According to André d'Allemagne, "Traditional Quebec nationalism has thus been reactionary and indifferent to social problems, which distinguishes it from today's 'neonationalism,' "[6] The other consequence of this state of affairs was that the overall domination of the French-Canadian nation for a long time prevented the workers from realizing that they were being exploited as a social class, conditioned as they were to react to the domination and colonization of the nation as a whole. When this burden of subordination is lifted, the workers of Quebec will find it all the easier to conquer the State, given the rickety character of our national bourgeoisie. As early as 1964, Fernand Dumont wrote: "The traditional ideology held that we had at the most only a petite bourgeoisie of our own, if not exclusively a middle class. A left-wing ideology might carry this observation to its logical conclusion, by advocating a social development which would leave out a constitution based on a national bourgeoisie, in order to base itself on elites already existing in our midst, but which do not yet possess a coordinating ideology. I am thinking of the militant workers; the militant farmers of the cooperative movements; the young civil servants of the State of Quebec; Ottawa civil servants who feel alienated in the framework of a federal administration; young technicians working for the great foreign companies."[7]

Since 1960, ethnic consciousness and class consciousness have developed along parallel lines. I myself wrote in 1965: "In the past, the ethnic consciousness of certain social strata inhibited the growth of class consciousness; today, however, as new social strata develop a national consciousness, other social elements acquire a stronger class consciousness. As the middle and upper classes struggle to appropriate the new State of Quebec, the classes below them develop their own plans to lay claim to the State and the nation. The battle against Ottawa concerns economic control and political power; it is not impossible that the wage-earning classes, using the same model, will go beyond their usual demands for higher pay and social security to wrestle with Quebec's ruling classes for control of the economy and collective power. We are in a turbulent period of Quebec's history, and it may be that the ethnic and social conflicts are in the process of overlapping and activating one another."[8]

Five years later, it is clear that this evolution has not taken the direct route we expected it to. Many developments have been marking time. We also realize that the forces which are determined to keep Quebec dependent have not been idle either. The money powers, abetted by their surest allies, the federalists, have made every effort to lull the national and class consciousness of the people of Quebec. The chambers of commerce, the great corporations and the federalists are waging a campaign all over the province, spending more and more money to halt the liberation movements, whether national or socioeconomic. The mass media gave extensive coverage to all the protest movements at the beginning of the Quiet Revolution. Today they are more sparing in their treatment; they pay more attention to the "forces of order."

On the other hand, flamboyant actions and declarations seem to have given way to movements and actions which are less spectacular but more efficient. In ever growing circles of the population, the ideology of 1960-1964 has yielded a keener and keener awareness of national and socioeconomic alienation. The first period, a time for new definitions of our situation, involved only the intelligentsia. Today, citizens' committees, trade union political action committees, and student groups in higher education (colleges and universities) are the places where consciousness arises and practical schemes are formulated. Less spectacular than the inflamed rhetoric or the bombs of the FLQ (*Front de Libération du Québec*), these movements are much more effective and are leading the people of Quebec more steadily towards socioeconomic and national liberation. Now that more and more Quebeckers know what kind of society they want, the struggle against Ottawa has diminished only to grow more intense in Quebec itself, between classes and social groups. The trade union movement is growing apace. "One of the most significant (and probably the most spectacular) phenomena of the social evolution of Quebec during the Quiet Revolution has undoubtedly been trade union penetration into occupational categories and wage-earning groups which, until the last few years, had been impermeable to this form of collective action." Professor Cardin adds,

"Quebec is not the only place that this development has occurred, but it is in Quebec that the phenomenon has acquired by far the greatest scope and expanded the most rapidly. We can speak indeed of 'revolution' where, in the last few years, the trade union idea has broken out of the framework imposed on it by our labour laws, inherited from the last World War, and has spread at a remarkable speed to groups which up to then looked upon it as taboo: engineers, professional people and civil servants."[9] Class relationships become more nakedly obvious as the veil concealing the nation's domination is torn away, and as the ranks of the separatists are swelled. The phenomenon is most clearly seen among young people and intellectuals.

Today, the question of Quebec is brought back to the strictly political level. More and more in agreement in our definition of Quebec and on the goals it must enshrine, we are asking ourselves what measures must be taken to achieve our ends. Soon the principal ideologies — of catching up and of surpassing — will confront each other on the electoral plane.

Decolonization and National Character

One of the most interesting effects of the Quiet Revolution is likely to go unnoticed, because it is a process rather than an event: the French-speaking people are gradually recovering their proper personality. This phenomenon is particularly noticeable in the artistic activities of the last few years. As often happens, the artists are the avant-garde of the liberation movement.

In a number of studies, Jacques Berque has shown that the domination of one society by another has effects which go beyond the social and economic realm. Whether we have to deal with depersonalization or cultural alienation, the results are the same; the dominated group tends to become profoundly inhibited and its national character tends to change. To use the language of the geneticist, the national traits become recessive, not only evident traits like language, social behaviour and customs, but the most latent and all-encompassing configurations of culture and personality. French Canadians possessed a culture tending towards the pole of what anthropologists call a "warm culture," extroverted and Dionysiac. In areas of prolonged contact with the Other, they had come to affect a kind of Apollonian personality; in their desire to put up a false front, they allowed this pseudopersonality to become second nature. We have a bizarre example of this in the little fellows of St. James Street (the Bay Street of Montreal). They dress in the English manner (complete with rolled umbrella), keep their face expressionless when they speak, and affect a stiff and starchy mien, to make people think that they, too, must be counted among the builders of the British Empire. As Quebeckers come to their senses, they become their old selves again, leaving the Other's umbrella in the vestibule. In the plastic arts, music, the popular song, architecture, ceramics and poetry, depersonalization is on the way out; the masks are falling.

"They are a colonial people," says Professor Berque in speaking of Quebeckers, "to the extent that their identity is reluctant to base itself on the folkloric and the residual, to which one would like to reduce them."[10] Once upon a time, in their docility, the French Canadians reduced themselves to that level. Today hardly anyone is abusing himself in this way, except for the federalists.

If Quebeckers do not want to be confined to the residual, the picturesque, the folkloric, where is the essential, the fundamental stuff of their culture? Some have felt that Quebec's long search for identity would lead to a kind of fundamental archaism; they would have only to recognize it and build their city of the future around it. Fernand Dumont gives somewhat this impression in quoting Paul Ricoeur, who wrote at the end of an article on Western civilization: "We must be progressive in politics but archaic in poetics." Dumont comments on Ricoeur: "To limit one's aims to giving everyone a certain security and an acceptable income is to place oneself in the mainstream of the old liberalism. One credits the individual with an ability to choose his values which he does not possess, unless he is confirmed by a certain consensus with other people. This consensus is archaic in two senses: it appeals to solidarities which have matured over a long period of time and it is lodged in the unconscious, where essential values and symbols interact. Archaism and progressivism — it's the meeting of poetry and technology, love and the family budget, human values and the planned economy."[11] Jacques Berque wonders about "Frenchness," what sort of reality will it reestablish? Perhaps I am being too hard on these two sociologists, but I am disturbed that they both seem to maintain that in every dormant culture there is a stable core of values and symbols which need only be reactivated once they have been discovered. What bothers me in the case of Quebec is that these old values are very closely linked with the traditional society and with a spirituality which is somewhat too "ultramontanist"; these things would not go very well with what we have become today, and especially not with what we want to become. For me, the essence of culture is contained not in values and synbols but in a nucleus of collective dispositions, in a "form" rather than a content, to use Berque's terminology. When a people thus exchanges its values and symbols for others, it marks the new acquisitions with its own peculiar stamp. As our national community matures, it will assimilate values and symbols which in their turn will supply the traits of our collective personality. We must discover and shape these values and these symbols in a collective action involving the participation of the greatest number of people. The consensus and the solidarities which have emerged in the course of our history are part of our national life, but they must not prejudice the modern culture that we have to build. I am pleading here in favour of an "open society" which nurtures life and is nurtured by it.

Whatever course it takes, Quebec is doomed to walk a dangerous tightrope. It must preserve the qualities of openness and freedom of action which it owes to its recent emergence on the international scene, and yet be faithful to those ancestors who managed to survive in this country of cold and snow. At the conclusion of the essay that I have quoted, Dumont writes: "Like many others of my generation, my choice is made — we have reached the age of jealous loyalties. I shall continue to live, love, dream, and write in French Canada. I don't quite know why; in any case, I shall not betray that obscure ideal which I have inherited from my illiterate ancestors. This ideal, vague though it may ever be, has revived in me that most disgraced of feelings, the sense of honour. Each age offers its own challenge; the task assumed by our ancestors was to survive so that their descendants, now and in the future, might set about building a world to embody their obscure dreams." Now we can speak for our forefathers, who were never called upon to speak for themselves. Our task, and the task of all those who have joined us, or soon will join us, in greater and greater numbers, is to build a Quebec culture which is open, dynamic and creative.

And Yet!

There is no real conclusion to our story. Quebec is an essentially shifting reality, and no one can predict what will happen here in the near future. At the moment federalists and separatists are involved in a fight to the finish. Each group is trying to find out if the direction of history will favour its choice; the separatists are pinning their hopes on the right to self-determination as proclaimed in several modern declarations of the rights of national collectivities. As for the federalists, they have all the arrogance of those who think they are walking hand in hand with history, because they have the illusion that they are making history. They profess that they are not interested in nineteenth-century problems; they say that in a world swept up in and unified by a powerful network of technology, anyone who talks of independence or national liberation shows a remarkable lack of understanding of present-day needs and problems. According to them, Quebec has missed out on the nineteenth century, and is therefore condemned to economic and cultural domination for life. Such is the so-called iron law of postindustrial society.

Marshall McLuhan is the great prophet of modernism. Big corporations, and even the Prime Minister of Canada, consult him to find out what the future holds in store for them. Strangely enough, McLuhan does not agree with the federalist predictions for the future of Quebec. According to him, the age of technology we live in favours psychic integration at the societal level, but tends, on the contrary, towards the decentralization and disaggregation of large political groupings. States like Canada, which were made of whole cloth in the nineteenth century to promote trade, are now in serious trouble. The technology of the day made political centralization a good idea at the time; today it is obsolete.

In a *Playboy* magazine interview of March 1969, Marshall McLuhan said in reference to examples of political disintegration: "... In my own country, the *Québecois* are in the first stages of a war of independence ... we've witnessed the collapse of several ambitiously unrealistic schemes for regional confederation." McLuhan predicted that the new states born of dissolved federations would not necessarily make war on one another, but might rather devote themselves to cultural cooperation.

Meanwhile, the federal politicians and the businessmen continue to practise what René Lévesque calls "economic terrorism." They predict the worst catastrophes if Quebec leaves the Canadian nest; they try to create an atmosphere of panic which would prevent the people of Quebec from deciding their future freely. They are well aware that the underdog is always afraid of losing the little he has managed to wrest from his master.

These men, who consider themselves "modern" and

"informed," do not realize that in the latter twentieth century there are social and cultural forms of domination and privation which are just as resented as economic underdevelopment. Today, who can buy enough votes to solve the Black problem, the youth problem or . . . the Quebec problem? The tricks that used to work in the city wards of North America, in the late nineteenth century, are today as outdated as the British monarchy, political bossism and Tammany Hall. It's astonishing that Trudeau's minister of propaganda hasn't heard about these things yet.

When all is said and done, Quebec's future will never be absolutely certain; even political independence would be only a beginning. We must realize that to be a *Québecois* is to agree to live dangerously.

Chapter 10
The Agonizing Steps to Freedom

At one time or other in their history, all nations have had to fight hard to achieve or maintain their independence, but the intensity and duration of this struggle have varied greatly from country to country. When Quebec finally wins its freedom, it will offer the example of a people who, never having known independence — as a French, British and Canadian colony, or as an economic satellite of the U.S.A. and Canada — needed two centuries to liberate themselves. The Quiet Revolution began in 1960, the two-hundredth anniversary of the British conquest.

Today, in November 1970, the military occupation of Quebec has been achieved by the Canadian army; civil liberties have been suspended and a state of war proclaimed. The government of Canada has taken the Quebec government under its wing; the latter has ceased to exist for all practical purposes, and has become a regional appendix of the Ottawa government. From the days of the 1969-1970 leadership campaign of the Quebec Liberal party, Robert Bourassa, who was to become premier of Quebec, renounced every thought of independence in relation to the government of Canada; he is pursued by his acts.

Since Thursday, October 15, 1970, when the Canadian Army occupied Quebec, and since the proclamation of the War Measures Act in the early hours of the following day, there have been thousands of house and personal searches, raids and seizures of documents of all kinds throughout Quebec. There have been more than 500 arrests without warrant. Poets, artists, professors, teachers, doctors, lawyers, workers, taxi drivers, students and technicians have been arrested and thrown into prison without any kind of charge being laid against them. Only the businessmen seem to have been spared.

How has Quebec come to find itself in such a situation? The first French edition of *Quebec in Question* was published in June 1969. At that time Trudeau had been in power since June 1968, and the great offensive against Quebec had been under way for a year. My aim in this chapter is to enumerate certain facts which seem to have contributed to the process begun by the elections of 1968, a process which has culminated in the terrorism of the FLQ and the violence of a military and police occupation. These two forms of violence engender one another and correspond to one another. In both camps, there has been a resort to tactics whose cost is borne by the people of Quebec.

We are concerned here with three most important events: the passage of Bill 63 following the St. Léonard crisis described in Chapter Eight of this book; the elections of April 29, 1970, which some have called "the coup d'état of April 29";[1] and finally, the occupation of Quebec by the Canadian Army, the immediate cause of which was the kidnapping of the British diplomat James Cross and of the Quebec cabinet minister Pierre Laporte, perpetrated by the *Front de Libération du Quebec* (FLQ), on October 5 and October 10, 1970.

To Be or Not to Be

In the last eighteen months, the general situation in Quebec has deteriorated. All the evils of a colonized and underdeveloped country have grown worse. There are from 150,000 to 170,000 unemployed (in a population of 6,000,000); there are more than 300,000 people on welfare; the standard of living is 27 per cent lower than that of Ontario and 50 per cent below that of the United States; Quebec is more heavily taxed and more in debt than any other part of North America: 38 per cent of the families of Montreal have an income of less than $4000 per year, and 25 per cent earn less than $3000. The only positive aspect of the situation is that Quebeckers are becoming more and more aware of their condition as an underdog, colonized people.

In the last few years, the French Canadians have become gradually more conscious of the fact that the problem of their colonial status and their underdevelopment could be solved, sooner or later, by their disappearance as a nation. Behind much of the agitation of the last few months we can see the most agonizing doubt that can beset a nation: whether or not it will continue to exist.

The high birthrate of the people of Quebec, which allowed them to grow rapidly in numbers from the time of their settlement in North America, has dropped drastically; "the 'revenge of the cradle' has passed into history. In 1951 the fertility of French Canadians was still 23 per cent higher than that of the rest of Canada, but in 1965 it was 5 per cent below the mean. Because of immigration from many countries of the world, which is unfavourable to us, and because of our declining birthrate, the percentage of French-speaking people in Canada is steadily diminishing. Another factor working against us is assimilation."[2]

In the preceding chapters, I have expressed the view that the assimilation of French-speaking people is irreversible outside of Quebec. This is also the conclusion reached by Robert Maheu in his demographic analysis: "(1) the number of French-speaking people has been declining, and will continue to decline in all provinces . . . (2) a reduction of the total number of French-speaking people living outside Quebec is very likely; this reduction could be very great . . . (3) in the past, the French-speaking people of Canada have been concentrated in Quebec; in the future, they will be more and more concentrated there. . . ."[3]

It seems that the fate of French-speaking people in Canada has been sealed, but what about the Quebeckers? According to the most optimistic thesis, French-speaking people will still constitute 81 per cent of the Quebec population in 1991. Even with this hypothesis, the most favourable to French-speaking people, it is predicted that the area outside of Montreal will become more solidly French-speaking, and Montreal more English-speaking than is the case today. According to the most pessimistic hypothesis — the worst is not certain, but it seems probable — the French-speaking people will not be more than 72 per cent of Quebec's population in 1991, i.e., probably less than 50 per cent in Montreal, the metropolis of Quebec. A great majority of Quebeckers have become aware that they must stop the process of assimilation at all costs, in Quebec itself, if they do not want to wind up in the same situation as the minorities in the rest of Canada, who are subjected to a relentless process of assimilation. Several groups, associations and individuals have demanded energetic measures to combat this from their government, and have insisted on the establishment of French unilingualism in Quebec.

Bill 63: A Mockery of Justice

On June 27, 1968, the St. Léonard school board adopted a regulation — "That in all classes of grade one of primary school under the jurisdiction of the school board of St. Léonard-de-Port-Maurice, as of September 1968, the language of instruction be French" — which caused an uproar in Quebec and in Canada. The government of Quebec, in the hands of the *Union Nationale* party, equivocated, made studies, asked for more time and did nothing. It was only in the fall of 1969 that the government, having withdrawn one bill, No. 85, tabled a second called Bill 63, which it called a "law to promote the French language in Quebec." Although the law at first appeared to favour the teaching of French by a number of means, it in no way solved the problem of the anglicization of the immigrants. Bill 63 aimed at "assuring that the English-speaking children of Quebec acquire a knowledge of the French language and that the persons who immigrate to Quebec acquire a knowledge of the French language and have their children instructed in this language"; on the other hand, however, *it gave to everyone the liberty of attending school in the language of his choice, and it obliged the school commissions to establish schools in accordance with the choices of the students.*

Henri Egretaud has written: "In sum, Bill 63 legalizes a certain number of situations which might well seem unjust:

 — individual rights outweigh collective rights and individual responsibility

 — the 'special status' of the English language is recognized, together with the 'privileges' attached to it

 — the status quo is preserved where French is concerned, contrary to what the Bill proclaims, except for the powers granted to the Office of the French Language."[4]

When this bill was tabled in the Quebec Assembly in October 1969, the people of Quebec demonstrated against it, as they have perhaps never demonstrated against anything before in their history. For almost two weeks Quebeckers went into the streets to protest against the government. There was a general strike of students in the educational establishments; high schools, CEGEPs,[5] universities. In every part of Quebec groups were organized to protest against Bill 63.

The people opposed to the bill and the demonstrators were organized by two popular leagues. The *Front du Québec français* (FQF) brought together hundreds of associations and groups such as the Confederation of Nation Trade Unions, the St. Jean Baptiste Society and the CEQ (*Corporation des Enseignants du Québec,* Quebec Teachers' Association). A second, more radical league was formed against Bill 63, consisting of the FLP (*Front de Libération Populaire,* Popular Liberation Front); the LSO (*La ligue socialiste ouvrière,* Socialist Workers' League); the MSP (*Mouvement syndical politique,* Political Trade Union Movement); and several workers' and citizens' committees. Thousands of people demonstrated in the streets and attended mass meetings (there were 50,000 people at one meeting in Montreal). Between 30,000 and 40,000 people marched on Quebec, the capital, to protest. All these demonstrations took place in an atmosphere of great festivity, of liberation, of a throwing off of inhibitions.

More than ever in the history of Quebec, the citizens mobilized in favour of the defense of their language. They had become more and more aware that the low status of their language was a reflection of their own inferior social and economic status. For the people of Quebec, October 1969 was an important step on the road to awareness, a necessary stage of their growing radicalization.

A few weeks later, the police force of Montreal went on strike. One newspaper headline said: "Montreal is Bloody and in Flames." Mobs of people went looting stores in the commercial districts. The Riot Act was read and the Canadian Army was moved in to replace the Montreal police. The strike was soon over and the army withdrew. Even then the eyes of the world were turned on Montreal, the metropolis of a country where violent upheavals were becoming more and more the rule.

The "Coup d'état" of April 29, 1970

The Quebec government emerged from the year 1969 anxious and divided. Premier Bertrand had taken up the reins of government and of his party after the death of Daniel Johnson, then premier of Quebec. At a leadership convention, Bertrand was able to win out over his minister of education only after a campaign of several weeks. Many saw Bertrand as a decent fellow, full of goodwill, but belonging to another age. He was an Uncle Tom, a well-behaved optimist who believed that with patience everything would work out. A man of sincerity and integrity, he was not equal to the merciless attacks that Ottawa was making on Quebec. Bertrand was being outmaneuvered at every turn. Cardinal, his minister of education, was much more aggressive and better equipped to fight Ottawa, and also more radical where Quebec-federal relations were concerned. He was supported for the leadership by the younger members of the *Union Nationale*, reformist or nationalist elements, and by some of the brains of the party, because in their eyes Cardinal would be a continuation of Johnson. In the voting for Bill 63, only two *Union Nationale* members of Parliament abstained: Jérôme Proulx and Antonio Flamard. The Liberal MPP Michaud also abstained. Only the two *Parti québecois* representatives René Lévesque and Jérôme Proulx (who went over to the PQ) voted against it.

An election was called by Bertrand a few months after the Bill 63 controversy. In the Canadian political system, as in England, elections are not held at regular intervals of time; the head of government takes the initiative in dissolving Parliament and calling an election. The government is elected for five years, but in practise elections are usually held every four years. The leader of the party in power, especially if he is favoured by the opinion polls, can try to foil his adversaries by calling elections when he thinks he can catch them off guard. Harold Wilson tried this tactic in England recently, but was defeated at the polls. Jean-Jacques Bertrand tried the same thing, and with the same results.

On the eve of the elections, the Liberal party, which had initiated the Quiet Revolution of 1960, seemed as divided as the *Union Nationale*. Jean Lesage had had to resign as leader at the end of 1969; he had been repeatedly attacked by certain federal Liberals who found him too pro-Quebec, and by Judge Wagner, a party strongman famous in Quebec's history as the hero of "the Saturday of the Nightsticks." (During the Queen's last visit to her French-Canadian vassals, in 1965, she had to be displayed to the people of Quebec City at a healthy distance. Several hundred policemen from different forces formed a human shock absorber between Her Majesty and her people. The most anti-British onlookers came near enough to the policemen to get beaten by their nightsticks. The great organizer of these festivities was the minister of justice at the time, Mr. Claude Wagner.)

In January 1970, the Quebec Liberal party thus had to elect a leader to replace Jean Lesage. There were three candidates for the job: Robert Bourassa, a member of the federal and provincial Liberal establishment; Pierre Laporte, a politician with expertise in backroom intrigue and the support of the greatest number of Quebec Liberal MPPs; and Claude Wagner, a strongman who was wooing the masses on a "law and order" platform. From the start, Bourassa was the most openly federalist. An accountant with a head for figures, he projected the image of a young functionalist and technocrat who is not encumbered by constitutional theories or ideologies. He said that he wanted to bring order into Quebec's economy; he promised 100,000 new jobs and hundreds of millions of dollars that he planned to borrow from his good friend Trudeau, the Prime Minister of Canada. He looked like the man who could inspire the confidence of the Americans and thereby persuade them to invest hundreds of millions in Quebec. He gave the impression of being honest, efficient and well-mannered. Laporte was the traditional Quebec politician. When he spoke to the people he used all the tricks in the book: phony amiability, Laporte as defender of the weak and the oppressed, Laporte as victim of the great and powerful. He had prepared his campaign far ahead, and had rallied to his cause all the party specialists in petty dealings and small ideas. Wagner, the third candidate, tried to bill himself as the friendly cop who has come to restore law and order. He had no program, no ideology, no ideas. He took himself for the Man of Destiny. The result: Bourassa won the leadership, Wagner came in second and Laporte third. Laporte rallied to the new leader; Wagner resigned from the Liberal party and was appointed judge by the *Union Nationale* government, at that time still in office. All the political parties began to think about the elections coming up in 1970.

The *Parti québecois*, founded in 1968, was frantically getting organized, and so successfully that it began to frighten everybody: federal politicians, Liberals and *Union Nationale* members. A party of the people, its success would depend on the devotion and on the financial resources of its members. The old parties were financed by secret "war chests" filled by individuals and institutions interested in buying the influence of political parties. These silent partners were not political partisans; for them, this was just another business deal. Several of these institutions contributed to the campaign funds of both traditional parties — Liberal and *Union Nationale* — in proportion to the odds on their winning the election. The Liberal party of Quebec was also helped, obviously, by its big brother, the Liberal party of Canada, which aided it in many important ways, but especially on April 29, 1970.

For the old parties, the election was a matter of selling the product. Money was no problem in their efforts to project the image of a party which would correspond to what the opinion polls had told them the people expected. The image, once formed, was then promoted by every means: speeches, television, radio, newspapers, and all manner of propaganda. The same advertising agencies were involved in selling political parties, soap and automobiles. There was scarcely any ideological difference between these two parties. In Quebec, one party was more or less pro-Ottawa or pro-Quebec; one party had more or less marketable candidates; one party had a more or less stable group of supporters. Given the hard times, the traditional supporters of the old parties still tended to drift away to the so-called new parties.

For a new party like the *Parti québecois*, the situation was very different. In the beginning, it could count on the support of only approximately 8 percent of the electorate who, in 1966, had voted for the RIN (*Rassemblement pour l'indépendance nationale*), and on a much smaller number who had voted for the RN (*Ralliement Nationale*), since the RIN and the RN had merged to form the *Parti québecois* in 1968. An ideological party with a highly structured socioeconomic and national program, it campaigned in the April 29 elections for an independent Quebec and for the formation of a kind of Common Market with Canada. Its domestic platform announced the most reformist social program in North America. The *Parti québecois* was not a traditional socialist party, but a party which, while retaining the essential features of capitalism, advocated serious social and economic reform.

Deprived of the means that high finance had offered to the old parties, the *Parti québecois* had to depend exclusively on the enthusiasm of its members. Organization and time were the crucial factors. In announcing premature elections, Bertrand had had the *Parti québecois* as much in mind as the Liberals. In many ways there was a kind of complicity between the old parties. In the beginning, the *Parti québecois* could hardly rely on any support from the English-speaking minority of Quebec (20 per cent of the electorate). This minority was very important, not only numerically but because it contained a large number of immigrants which the English-speaking establishment had attracted into its orbit. The *Parti québecois* thus had to try to appeal to the greatest possible number of those who had decided in favour of English-speaking culture, but who received very minimal benefits from the exploitation of Quebec. From many points of view, most of these immigrants — 80 per cent assimilated to the English-Canadian minority in Quebec — as well as the English-speaking "poor whites" were as much the victims of American and Canadian capitalism as the French-speaking people. Because of all these ethnic parameters, the overall strategy of the *Parti québecois* oscillated between two general schemes: either to try to win over only the French-speaking population of Quebec to the idea of independence, or to try to persuade all the residents of Quebec that this policy would be good for them. In the last elections, the PQ opted for the second strategy.

The elections of April 29 involved a fourth party which, though not much talked about, was to prove a disturbing influence of some importance. The Social Credit party had established itself many years before in Quebec, and until recently had limited itself to federal politics. Led by a man of the people from eastern Quebec, Réal Caouette, this party presented itself as the champion of the lower classes and won support in many of the poorer areas of the province. In the last ten years it has occasionally managed to get one of its men elected to the federal parliament from one of the cities of the hinterland; Quebec City and Sherbrooke are examples. It has never had any success in Montreal or in the Montreal area, which contains almost half of Quebec's population. Its supporters are concentrated in the rural areas, and its relative strength is above all due to the personality of its leader, Réal Caouette. Caouette is an orator who has the ear of the people; he has a redoubtable flair for simplification and a personal style which smacks of the village storyteller and the charlatan. Social Credit draws its strength from its tenacity and its powerful organization in the counties where it has some support. It has for many years engaged in continual door-to-door canvassing, even when there are no elections in the offing.

It is not easy to paint a clear picture of Social Credit's programs and ideas, especially for a public living outside Quebec. The doctrine of Social Credit goes back to the theories of a Scotsman, Major Douglas, who held that all the evils of our society were attributable to the fact that the issuing of money and credit is in the hands of financiers and bankers who never reissue the interest on the capital they have lent. The issuing of money and credit ought to be in the hands of the government of each country, and guaranteed by its natural resources and gross national product. In this scheme, each citizen would receive a social dividend paid out from the year-end balance of the country. At this level, Social Credit propaganda is directed against monopolies, banks, financiers — in a word, the "sharks of high finance." Given these premises, one would naturally expect Social Credit to be left-wing. Paradoxically, the doctrine of Social Credit has given birth, not only in Quebec but in Canada, to parties which may be described in general terms as right-wing or even extreme right-wing. Professional anticommunists and antisocialists, the Social Crediters are everywhere supported by the most socially and intellectually reactionary forces in the country. In the Canadian West, notably in Alberta where a Social Credit government has been in power for over thirty years, the leaders of the party are also very active members of their church congregations. In Quebec, a subgroup of Social Credit has so intimately mingled party doctrine and Catholic religion that it is impossible to say where one leaves off and the other begins.

Social Credit entered Quebec provincial politics for the first time in the elections of April 29. The Social Credit members of the Ottawa Parliament, although part of the Opposition, regularly support the Trudeau government and have for many years been uncompromising federalists. Many political observers feel that the Liberal party of Canada, federally in power with Trudeau, did much to encourage the Social Crediters to get mixed up in Quebec politics. As the Bertrand government had been in power since 1966, it was necessary to weaken it on the Right by presenting candidates who would cut into the rural adherents of the *Union Nationale* and would attract the federalist voters whom Robert Bourassa, leader of the Quebec Liberals, could not rally himself because of the discredit attached to the old parties in the eyes of many Quebec voters. Given the vogue for the "new" *Parti québecois,* it was necessary to counter it by introducing Social Credit into Quebec politics, where it could assume the guise of a new party.

The elections of April 29, 1970, are of fundamental importance. For the first time since the Rebellion of 1837, Quebeckers had a chance to elect a party which openly endorsed independence. To the right of the PQ were two strictly federalist parties, the Liberal party and Social Credit. Between these two was the *Union Nationale,* in power since 1966. The election was above all a contest between the Liberal party, the most powerful federalist party, and the PQ; these two organizations were much more in the public eye than the two rurally-based parties. The Liberal party enjoyed all the advantages that money and power can buy; the *Parti québecois* relied on the driving energy of its adherents and on the hope, soon to be justified, that devotion, greater imagination and more ingenuity could nullify the advantages of the Liberals' money. As for the *Union Nationale,* divided and fallen between two stools, its campaign scarcely got off the ground, the impression being that it had been sabotaged from within while rivals in the party stabbed each other in the back. As the election campaign progressed and the *Parti québecois* found increasing favour in the eyes of the people, the federal politicians, English Canadians and financiers appeared to grow more anxious, more irritable.

As the elections grew near, low blows were rained on the *Parti québecois.* The English-speaking federalist establishment had been seized with panic, and had made up their minds to resort to moral violence. The great majority of French-speaking Quebeckers seemed ready to vote for independence as long as they could be sure it wouldn't cost them much. It was decided to attack them through their hesitations about the economic consequences of independence. Economic terrorism entered the picture. Pierre Laporte, candidate in Chambly county (71.6 per cent French-speaking), had phony dollars printed which had a face value of only 65 cents, and distributed them widely among the people. These fictitious dollars signified that the standard of living in Quebec would drop 35 per cent if the PQ were elected. The English-Canadian establishment circulated rumours to the effect that capital was fleeing the province; arrangements were made to photograph eight Brinks armoured trucks supposedly leaving

Quebec for Ontario with millions of dollars' worth of securities aboard. This has since become known as "the Brinks coup." The federal politicians published a form of doctored balance sheet in which they tried to prove that if Quebec became independent it would lose hundreds of millions of dollars in revenue annually.

All these last-minute blows were widely publicized by the information media (the property of the establishment), and struck terror into the hearts of the little cheese-parers and the good folk who, already grappling with poverty, were fearful of the morrow. How many votes did the establishment gain by these tactics? Without a doubt, several tens of thousands at least.

On the night of April 29, election day, the results of the balloting were as follows: the Liberals obtained 72 seats in the provincial Assembly with 44 per cent of the popular vote; the PQ obtained 7 seats with 24 per cent of the vote; the *Union Nationale* got 18 seats with 20 per cent of the vote; and Social Credit 12 seats with 11 per cent. We can explain these anomalous results in several ways. With the electoral system of one person voting for a single candidate, the popular vote is not at all reflected in the final distribution of seats. Moreover, Quebec's electoral map gives greater electoral weight to the rural districts than to the urban areas. Since the strength of the PQ is above all in the cities, we might have expected it to be at a disadvantage from that point of view. These are defects inherent in our electoral system and in our electoral map. The British North America Act is the basic constitutional law of Canada. Because of it, twelve of Quebec's electoral districts,[6] which had a majority of English-speaking people when the act was proclaimed in 1867, cannot be revised without the consent of all the members of Parliament for these districts. These are rural districts, small in comparison to the city wards, and still inhabited by a certain proportion of English-speaking people. These districts were another handicap for the *Parti québecois*.

There was a fundamental injustice in the elections of

April 29, 1970. Given the electoral system and the electoral distribution, the English-speaking people (20 per cent of the electorate), who voted almost exclusively for the Liberal party, practically singlehandedly guaranteed the election of Bourassa to power. Bernard Smith has shown this in his book. In the electoral districts where there is a majority of English-speaking people, the majorities of votes won by the Liberals are the greatest by far of all the majorities won by them in Quebec. The French-speaking vote was everywhere divided, while the English-speaking population voted en masse for the Liberal party. In every electoral district where English-speaking people were a significant minority, they tipped the balance in favour of the Liberal party. "The English-speaking people of Quebec, be they rich or poor, right-wing or left-wing, new arrivals or old residents, from Montreal or outside of Montreal, male or female, educated or not, voted violently and en bloc against the independence of Quebec."[7] Bernard Smith says, "We recall that the *Suburban*[8] invited its 100,000 readers to start a civil war in the case of a victory by the *Parti québecois,* yet there was no protest on the part of the *Montreal Star,* the *Gazette,*[9] the Canadian Jewish Congress (always on the lookout for 'hate propaganda'), or, obviously, our own national P.E.T."[10]

After such results, it is clear that even the liberal spirits of Quebec's English-speaking minority are obtuse and given to panic. In South Africa and in Rhodesia the English-speaking liberals conduct themselves much better. Why have our liberals reacted like some solid phalanx of *pieds noirs*[11] who are being menaced, besieged and hunted down? The very age of the colonial situation in Quebec has inhibited, in our English-speaking liberals, the old Whig reflexes which in England sometimes operated in our favour, in the darkest days of the post-Conquest period.

After the elections of April 29, Hugh MacLennan, a Canadian novelist of international reputation, published his comments in the *Toronto Daily Star.* Whoever reads his article must surely feel that whatever arguments and statistics are brought forward in defense of the separatist thesis, the English-Canadian position will never change a jot. The English Canadians seem to be locked into a kind of maudlin romanticism. In the eyes of all the colonial masters of the world, none of the peoples they rule is fit for independence. Should the English Canadians ever cease to be the dominant minority in Quebec, it would, in their view, be the end of culture, of civilization, of the West, perhaps of the world. Should their domination cease, we the natives would be menaced by yet more dreadful perils. One would think they ruled us from philanthropic motives.

Despite all the precautions they had taken to ensure the defeat of the *Parti québecois,* the English Canadians were still very uneasy. Hugh MacLennan described this anxiety in his *Toronto Star* article of May 2, 1970. The English Canadians were talking among themselves of the end of the Weimar Republic, and René Lévesque seemed to them a veritable Hitler. "Men nearing retirement," he wrote, "spent sleepless nights worrying about what would happen to their pensions." The hospitals and universities were not sure what their future would be under a PQ regime. Did the novelist and his friends imagine that we were going to close the hospitals and the universities to embark on a joyous campaign of massacre? When hysteria grips a community whose privileges seem menaced, God knows what nightmares those people can have. The only atrocity MacLennan left out was the rape of English-speaking girls; there are still some things a gentleman does not discuss in public. "Half an hour after the polls closed," he wrote, "everyone knew that Quebec, in the last five minutes of the 12th hour, had opted for security." And for unemployment, slums, low wages, and humiliations! The English Canadians of Quebec and the Trudeau-Caouette axis had done their work well.

Once the nightmare had ended, MacLennan and his people could hardly contain themselves for joy. What would they do now? As MacLennan told us, they were going to rush to the defense of the ecology of the biosphere by attacking Washington's policies in the Arctic. Who could have put it better? I doubt that the South Africans or the Rhodesians have ever carried moral doublethink to quite that extreme. Some of the latter have had the honesty to admit that they are frightened because they find their privileges threatened — privileges, that is, of dominating the majority which they have arrogated to themselves. It seems that as our English-speaking citizens grow more frightened, their moral and humanitarian objectives grow more grandiose, but also more distant from the concerns of everyday life. When independence finally comes, the ecology of the biosphere will remain to occupy the English-speaking establishment in Quebec. That will be the end of a long story — and the beginning of another.

October in Quebec

Despite the Liberal victory of April 29, the federalists of the Montreal establishment did not devote all their time, as Hugh MacLennan had suggested, to the defense of the biosphere. A closer scrutiny of the election results showed that one French-speaking Quebecker in three had become a separatist, and that by adding the PQ's 24 per cent of the popular vote to the 20 per cent for the *Union Nationale,* one obtained approximately the same percentage of votes as those won by the federalist Bourassa (44 per cent). Especially where French Canadians are concerned, one can never be sure of anything. A little electoral reform, a bit more popular discontent, and one day one wakes up to an independent Quebec. In a democracy, troops are never sent to crush a people who have expressed their wishes at the polls; it was therefore necessary to work to destroy this possibility of independence in the egg. This imperative was made all the stronger by the weakness of the Bourassa government. Unconditionally federalist but lacking in real statesmen, it had at the most two or three good technocrats. Things could get really rough; the campaign against Quebec had to be intensified. Trudeau had been elected to "put Quebec in its place," and he felt that he had to finish the job as soon as possible. While the good Bourassa was out hunting for jobs and capital, Trudeau and his functionalist team were developing the strategies made possible by their money and their power.

In Montreal, the metropolis of Quebec, events had taken a new turn. I have remarked in an earlier chapter[12] that the time for new definitions of our situation, involving only the intelligentsia, had come to an end; the citizens themselves were joining the struggle. However men come to examine their colonial situation, through ideology or through an awareness of the concrete conditions of life imposed on them as colonized people, they all arrive, eventually, at programs and actions in favour of national and socioeconomic liberation. This is what began to happen all over Quebec, but especially in Montreal. In early 1970, FRAP (*Le Front d'action politique,* League for Political Action) was born. An organization comprising citizens' groups, militants, trade union groups and students attending CEGEP's and universities, FRAP decided not only to make a critical attack on the municipal governments of Montreal, but also to form a political party intended to give wage-earners a chance to take over at City Hall. "Power to the Wage-Earners" was the slogan of this people's action league.

For the last ten years, the municipal government of Montreal had been run by people who were not wage-earners. Of the 52 councillors of the ruling Civic party, 31 were merchants, brokers or businessmen; 19 were manufacturers or professional people; one was an office clerk, and one an electrician.

One man ruled the Civic party — Mr. Jean Drapeau, who chose candidates and ran the party as he saw fit. His loyal subordinate, Lucien Saulnier, was chairman of the executive committee. These two strongmen and their select group of 52 councillors administered an annual budget of 300 million dollars. Opposition was nonexistent. In the municipal elections of 1966, only 33 per cent of the registered voters bothered to go to the polls. Not only was there no opposition at City Hall, but in the opinion of the mayor of Montreal, there was no need for one; he is said to have remarked: "What could they be opposed to?" In 1969, Drapeau and Saulnier realized that citizens' committees and other groups — those in fact which gave birth to FRAP — were forming a people's opposition to their regime. In a violent denunciation of these organizations to Ottawa, they demanded the appointment of a Royal Commission to investigate the suspicious conduct of certain persons. The federal governemnt had not completely lost its head at that point and did not feel particularly threatened. It therefore rejected the alarmist statements of the two witch-hunters and sent them packing. Drapeau and Saulnier still continued to compile dossiers on subversive citizens, i.e., those who showed some tendency to oppose their regime. The first congress of FRAP was held on August 28, 1970, and the opening address was given by Pierre Vadeboncoeur, in the 1950's a prime mover of the review *Cité Libre* and a colleague of P.-E. Trudeau. Vadeboncoeur declared in part: "This platform is one of the most remarkable political documents that have been produced in Quebec for many years. It is as remarkable for its soundness and its earnestness, for the information in contains, and for its realism and honesty of purpose, as for the fact that it has been inspired by a profound desire to help the people; FRAP, indeed, is the result of political action in the working-class districts over the last seven years or so."[13]

Since April 28, 1970, FRAP had been organizing for the mayoralty elections, scheduled for October 25, 1970. FRAP and Drapeau were to find themselves in the middle of the events which have shattered Quebec since October 5, 1970.

Terrorism

The citizens' committees had been active for almost seven years; terrorism had also been around in Quebec for about the same length of time. These two very different strategies had the same goal: the decolonization of Quebec. While the citizens' committees attacked the economic exploitation which had made the French Canadians second-class citizens in their own country, terrorists fought, in the beginning, against the political domination of Quebec by Canada.

Since 1963, hardly a year has gone by without some terrorist activity to remind us all that a "war of independence" is in progress in Quebec. The FLQ (*Front de libération du Québec*, Quebec Liberation Front) or, on another occasion, the ALQ (*L'armée de la libération du Québec*, the Quebec Liberation Army) stole weapons, perpetrated holdups, and made several bombing attacks. Dismantled one year, the FLQ reappeared the next with a new membership and new cells. Little by little, terrorism became a part of the Quebec way of life. The terrorists first struck against federal institutions and the English-speaking community. Later on, they became more aware of social and economic problems, and began to aim at French-Canadian establishments as well. In 1966, for example, a French-Canadian company was the target of a bombing attack. Pierre Vallières and Charles Gagnon, the best-known of the supposed FLQ members, were indicted for complicity in this affair but were acquitted and released in 1970. Their writings, such as Vallières' *Les Nègres blancs d'Amérique* (White Niggers of America), unquestionably reveal a turningpoint in the evolution of the FLQ. In its early days a nationalist organization, the FLQ gradually became more aware of the economic stranglehold on Quebec and began to direct its actions as much against North American capitalism as against Ottawa's political control. As it developed, the FLQ began to attract people from all levels of society, especially young people.

Kidnapping as a Pressure Technique

At 8.30 a.m. on October 5, 1970, the diplomat James Cross was kidnapped from his luxurious residence in west Montreal at the point of a submachine gun. The FLQ immediately issued a communiqué in which it admitted to having kidnapped Cross and set out its conditions for his release. From the beginning, the FLQ showed great skill in drawing the press, radio and televison into the middle of things. Its communiqués, addressed to the Montreal radio stations CKAC and CKLM, were deposited in trashcans and other public places; the radio stations were told by telephone where to find the messages, which they subsequently broadcast. For ten days, from October 5 to October 16, when Ottawa declared a "state of apprehended insurrection" and sent the army to occupy Quebec, the mass media were constantly in the limelight. Quebec became one great land of broadcasting units and receiving stations; information was king. For the first time, perhaps, in the history of Quebec, information was transmitted without hindrance. Quebec had become one vast communications network.

The FLQ at first made many demands in exchange for Cross' freedom: the broadcasting of the FLQ manifesto by all the radio and television stations, and its publication in the newspapers; the freeing of twenty-three FLQ prisoners; a safe-conduct to Algeria or Cuba for all the prisoners and all the cells that had participated in the kidnapping of Cross; payment of 500,000 dollars in gold ingots; publication by the government of the name and the photograph of the informer who had brought about the arrest of an earlier FLQ group; an end to police searches. The government agreed to the first demand. The manifesto was read over the CBC radio and television networks, and was widely published by the press. The complete text of this manifesto is as follows:

FLQ Manifesto

The people in the *Front de Libération du Québec* are neither Messiahs nor modern-day Robin Hoods. They are a group of Quebec workers who have decided to do everything they can to assure that the people of Quebec take their destiny into their own hands, once and for all.

The *Front de Libération du Québec* wants total independence for Quebeckers; it wants to see them united in a free society, a society purged for good of its gang of rapacious sharks, the big bosses who dish out patronage and their henchmen, who have turned Quebec into a private preserve of cheap labour and unscrupulous exploitation.

The *Front de Libération du Québec* is not an aggressive movement, but a response to the aggression organized by high finance through its puppets, the federal and provincial governments (the Brinks farce, Bill 63, the electoral map, the so-called "social progress" (sic) tax, the Power Corporation, medical insurance — for the doctors, the guys at Lapalme . . .).

The *Front de Libération du Québec* finances itself through voluntary (sic) taxes levied on the enterprises that exploit the workers (banks, finance companies, etc. . . .).

"The money powers of the status quo, the majority of the traditional tutors of our people, have obtained from the voters the reaction they hoped for, a step backwards rather than the changes we have worked for as never before, the changes we will continue to work for" (René Lévesque, April 29, 1970).

Once, we believed it worthwhile to channel our energy and our impatience, in the apt words of René Lévesque, into the *Parti Québecois,* but the Liberal victory shows that what is called democracy in

Quebec has always been, and still is, nothing but the "democracy" of the rich. In this sense the victory of the Liberal party is in fact nothing but the victory of the Simard-Cotroni election-fixers. Consequently, we wash our hands of the British parliamentary system; the *Front de Libération du Québec* will never let itself be distracted by the electoral crumbs that the Anglo-Saxon capitalists toss into the Quebec barnyard every four years. Many Quebeckers have realized the truth and are ready to take action. In the coming year Bourassa is going to get what's coming to him: 100,000 revolutionary workers, armed and organized!

Yes, there are reasons for the Liberal victory. Yes, there are reasons for poverty, unemployment, slums, for the fact that you, Mr. Bergeron of Visitation Street, and you too, Mr. Legendre of Ville de Laval, who make $10,000 a year, do not feel free in our country, Quebec.

Yes, there are reasons, the guys who work for Lord know them, and so do the fishermen of the Gaspé, the workers on the North Shore; the miners who work for Iron Ore, for Q-UeBEC Cartier Mining, for Noranda know these reasons too. The honest workingmen at Cabano, the guys they tried to screw still one more time, they know lots of reasons.

Yes, there are reasons why you, Mr. Tremblay of Panet Street and you, Mr. Cloutier who work in construction in St. Jérôme, can't afford "Golden Vessels" with all the jazzy music and the sharp decor, like Drapeau the aristocrat, the guy who was so concerned about slums that he had coloured billboards stuck up in front of them so that the rich tourists couldn't see us in our misery.

Yes, Madame Lemay of St. Hyacinthe, there are reasons why you can't afford a little junket to Florida like the rotten judges and members of Parliament who travel on our money.

The good workers at Vickers and at Davie Shipbuilding, the ones who were given no reason for being thrown out, know these reasons; so do the guys at Murdochville that were smashed only because they wanted to form a union, and whom the rotten judges forced to pay over two million dollars because they had wanted to exercise this elementary right. The guys of Murdochville are familiar with this justice; they know lots of reasons.

Yes, there are reasons why you, Mr. Lachance of St. Marguerite Street, go drowning your despair, your bitterness, and your rage in Molson's horse piss. And you, the Lachance boy, with your marijuana cigarettes. . . .

Yes, there are reasons why you, the welfare cases, are kept from generation to generation on public assistance. There are lots of reasons, the workers for Domtar at Windsor and East Angus know them; the workers for Squibb and Ayers, for the Quebec Liquor Commission and for Seven-up and for Victoria Precision, and the blue collar workers of Laval and of Montreal and the guys at Lapalme know lots of reasons.

The workers at Dupont of Canada know some reasons too, even if they will soon be able to express them only in English (thus assimilated, they will swell the number of New Quebeckers, the immigrants who are the darlings of Bill 63).

These reasons ought to have been understood by the policemen of Montreal, the system's muscle; they ought to have realized that we live in a terrorized society, because without their force and their violence, everything fell apart on October 7.

We've had enough of a Canadian federalism which penalizes the dairy farmers of Quebec to satisfy the requirements of the Anglo-Saxons of the Commonwealth; which keeps the honest taxi drivers of Montreal in a state of semi-slavery by shamefully protecting the exclusive monopoly of the nauseating Murray Hill, and its owner — the murderer Charles Hershorn and his son Paul who, the night of October 7, repeatedly tore a .22 rifle out of the hands of his employees to fire on the taxi drivers and thereby mortally wounded Corporal Dumas, killed as a demonstrator. Canadian federalism pursues a reckless import policy, thereby throwing out of work the people who earn low wages in the textile and shoe industries, the most downtrodden people in Quebec, and all to line the pockets of a handful of filthy "money-makers" in Cadillacs. We are fed up with a federalism which classes the Quebec nation among the ethnic minorities of Canada.

We, and more and more Quebeckers too, have had it with a government of pussy-footers who perform a hundred and one tricks to charm the American millionaires, begging them to come and invest in Quebec, the Beautiful Province where thousands of square miles of forests full of game and of lakes full of fish are the exclusive property of these all-powerful lords of the twentieth century. We are sick of a government in the hands of a hypocrite like Bourassa who depends on Brinks armoured trucks, an authentic symbol of the foreign occupation of Quebec, to keep the poor Quebec "natives" fearful of that poverty and unemployment to which we are so accustomed.

We are fed up with the taxes we pay that Ottawa's agent in Quebec would give to the English-speaking bosses as an "incentive" for them to speak French, to negotiate in French. Repeat after me: "Cheap labour is *main d'oeuvre à bon marché* in French."

We have had enough of promises of work and of prosperity, when in fact we will always be the diligent servants and bootlickers of the big shots, as long as there is a Westmount, a Town of Mount Royal, a

Hampstead, an Outremont, all these veritable fortresses of the high finance of St. James Street and Wall Street; we will be slaves until Quebeckers, all of us, have used every means, including dynamite and guns, to drive out these big bosses of the economy and of politics, who will stoop to any action however base, the better to screw us.

We live in a society of terrorized slaves, terrorized by the big bosses, Steinberg, Clark, Bronfman, Smith, Neopole, Timmins, Geoffrion, J. L. Lévesque, Hershorn, Thompson, Nesbitt, Desmarais, Kierans (next to these, Rémi Popol the Nightstick, Drapeau the Dog, the Simards' Simple Simon and Trudeau the Pansy are peanuts!).

We are terrorized by the Roman Capitalist Church, though this is less and less true today (who owns the square where the Stock Exchange was built?); terrorized by the payments owing to Household Finance, by the advertising of the grand masters of consumption, Eaton's, Simpson's, Morgan's, Steinberg's, General Motors . . .; terrorized by those exclusive clubs of science and culture, the universities, and by their boss-directors Gaudry and Dorais, and by the vice-boss Robert Shaw.

There are more and more of us who know and suffer under this terrorist society, and the day is coming when all the Westmounts of Quebec will disappear from the map.

Workers in industry, in mines and in the forests! Workers in the service industries, teachers, students and unemployed! Take what belongs to you, your jobs, your determination and your freedom. And you, the workers at General Electric, you make your factories run; you are the only ones able to produce; without you, General Electric is nothing!

Workers of Quebec, begin from this day forward to take back what is yours; take yourselves what belongs to you. Only you know your factories, your machines, your hotels, your universities, your unions; do not wait for some organization to produce a miracle.

Make your revolution yourselves in your neighbourhoods, in your places of work. If you don't do it yourselves, other usurpers, technocrats or someone else, will replace the handful of cigar-smokers we know today and everything will have to be done all over again. Only you are capable of building a free society.

We must struggle not individually but together, till victory is obtained, with every means at our disposal, like the Patriots of 1837-1838 (those whom Our Holy Mother Church hastened to excommunicate, the better to sell out to British interests).

In the four corners of Quebec, may those who have been disdainfully called lousy Frenchmen and alcoholics begin a vigorous battle against those who have muzzled liberty and justice; may they put out of commission all the professional holdup artists and swindlers: bankers, businessmen, judges and corrupt political wheeler-dealers. . . .

We are Quebec workers and we are prepared to go all the way. With the help of the entire population, we want to replace this society of slaves by a free society, operating by itself and for itself, a society open on the world.

Our struggle can only be victorious. A people that has awakened cannot long be kept in misery and contempt.

Long live Free Quebec!

Long live our comrades the political prisoners!

Long live the Quebec Revolution!

Long live the *Front de Libération du Québec*!

When the manifesto was broadcast and published, Cross was still alive and the governments were negotiating with the FLQ. No irremediable step had yet been taken. In an atmosphere of supercharged excitement, the manifesto was apparently well received by a large number of the people of Quebec. A federal cabinet minister was of the opinion that the people of Quebec would embark on a vast search for Cross and his kidnappers, but instead they found the terrible suspense exciting and became willing spectators of the conflict. On radio "hot lines," a high proportion of listeners said that they agreed with the FLQ analysis of the Quebec situation and with its overall objectives, the total liberation of Quebec. Almost everyone said that they were against violence, however. This response was what the federal politicians later referred to as the erosion of public opinion.

During the week ending Saturday, October 10, the FLQ handed out ultimatums to the government and threatened to execute Cross at a prescribed hour unless its demands were met. The FLQ established new execution dates when the government refused to give in and the negotiations dragged on, thereby giving the impression that it would never kill Cross. The Premier of Quebec is reported to have said: "These are local boys; they can't execute Cross."

On Saturday, October 10, Quebec's Minister of Justice, Jérôme Choquette, a lantern-jawed heavyweight, read a declaration, with the blessing of the government of Canada, to the effect that there would be no deals. A half-hour later, the FLQ struck back by kidnapping Choquette's colleague Pierre Laporte, Labour Minister in the Bourassa cabinet; the agonizing crisis intensified.

The following day, the Premier of Quebec, Robert Bourassa, made a pathetic and ambiguous speech, in which he hinted that the government of Quebec might be willing to negotiate with the FLQ. He appeared to be in an impossible situation, caught as he was between Ottawa's hard line and Drapeau's ultrahard line. The text of Bourassa's speech follows:

Bourassa's Statement

The stability of our political institutions is menaced by events which are exceptional and unprecedented in our province. What makes these actions both fundamentally unjust and extremely dangerous is the fact that we live in a place where freedom of expression and action is one of the greatest of all the countries of the world.

Even the political parties who question the political system itself have every liberty to express themselves. Moreover, in the last few years, people have not failed to use this freedom of expression to spread hatred and lies systematically.

The government cannot, must not and will not remain idle when the well-being of the individual is threatened at its very roots. I am too proud of being a Quebecker not to express to you my resolution and that of the government I lead to surmount this most serious crisis.

In this effort to safeguard the fundamental values of our civilization, I am sure that I have the support of all the elected representatives of the people, and I ask everybody to remain calm and confident in these difficult circumstances.

Are not, in fact, the merits of our people, their exceptional industriousness, their respect for others, their sense of liberty the best assurance of the victory of justice and peace?

This basic truth which, all things considered, should reassure us, must not make us forget, however, the extremely pressing difficulties confronting us, in which the lives of two persons are at stake: a typical Quebec politician devoted to the progress of his community, and a distinguished diplomat who has no part in the tensions which afflict our society.

In this connection, the *Front de Libération du Québec* has issued a communiqué demanding the whole and complete acceptance of their seven demands. Moreover, the Minister of Labour has sent me a letter in which he deals with two problems, police searches and the liberation of political prisoners.

Need we mention that we all value the lives of Mr. Laporte and Mr. Cross? Fate, in a rare example of its cruelty, decreed that the maintenance of public order should place their lives in jeopardy. It is because we truly value the lives of Mr. Laporte and Mr. Cross that, before discussing the fulfillment of the demands that have been made, we wish to establish procedures which would guarantee, to take the example referred to by Mr. Pierre Laporte, that the liberation of political prisoners would save the lives of the two hostages.

This is a preliminary arrangement that simple good sense forces us to demand, and it is on these terms that we ask the kidnappers to enter into communication with us.

How indeed could we agree to these demands without being assured that the other half of the agreement be fulfilled? The government of Quebec believes that it would be acting irresponsibly towards the State, and towards Mr. Laporte and Mr. Cross, if it did not insist on these precautions.

We wish to save the lives of Mr. Laporte and Mr. Cross. It is because we want this with all our heart that we make this offer.

My dear fellow-citizens; a great statesman once said: "To govern is to choose." We ourselves have chosen individual and collective justice.

As for myself, I will fight for this justice with all the means at my disposal, assuming all the risks, whatever they may be, that are necessary to assure the future of our people.

The next day, Monday, October 12, the government of Quebec appointed a negotiator, the lawyer Robert

Demers, as their representative; the FLQ chose Robert Lemieux, a lawyer who had acted on behalf of Vallières, Gagnon and other political prisoners. The negotiations did not really get off the ground. On Tuesday, rumours began to circulate in trade union, political and intellectual circles to the effect that the government of Canada was about to put Quebec under its protection and occupy the province militarily.

A group of Quebec personalities, aware of a slight breach between the position of the Ottawa government and that of Quebec, decided to come to the aid of their government and to make a determined effort to save the lives of the two hostages. Several Quebec citizens' groups supported "the sixteen."

The following is the press release of these "personalities," with their names:

Declaration of the "Sixteen"

The Cross-Laporte affair is above all a Quebec drama. One of the two hostages is a citizen of Quebec, the other a diplomat whose function temporarily made him a citizen of this province, with the same rights to the respect of his life and of his human dignity as each one of us.

The FLQ people, on the other hand, are a group on the fringes of this same Quebec society, but still constitute a part of our reality, for extremism belongs to the social organism, even if it indicates ill health and puts society in mortal danger.

We have reflected upon the fate of these two human lives, the collective reputation and honour of our society, and the real risk it is now running of social and political degradation. All these considerations make clear to us the fact that the primary responsibility for finding a solution and applying it must rest with Quebec.

The attitudes of certain people outside Quebec,

of which the latest and most incredible is that of Premier Robarts of Ontario, have contributed to the atmosphere of rigidity, almost military already, which one perceives in Ottawa. This situation threatens to reduce Quebec and its government to a tragic impotence. We must make a superhuman effort to agree to negotiate and to compromise. On this level, we believe that Quebec and its government really have the moral mandate and the responsibility, the knowledge of the facts and of the political climate necessary to come to an informed decision.

We feel this urgency all the more strongly because we fear, from certain quarters outside Quebec especially, the terrible temptation of embracing a political stance favouring the worst, i.e., the illusion that a chaotic and thoroughly ravaged Quebec would at last be easy to control, by any means whatever.

Setting aside the differences of opinion we may have on a great variety of subjects, aware only of the fact that at this moment we are all Quebeckers and thus vitally involved in the matter, we insist on giving our entire support to the intentions expressed by the Bourassa government on Sunday night; essentially, we most urgently recommend negotiations to exchange the two hostages for political prisoners — these negotiations must be made in the teeth of all objections from those outside Quebec, which necessarily will require the help of the federal government.

We urgently request all the citizens who share our point of view to make their opinions known publicly as soon as possible.

The signatories to the declaration are:

René Lévesque, president of the *Parti québecois*

Alfred Rouleau, president of the Desjardins Life Insurance Company

Marcel Pépin, president of the CSN (*Fédération canadienne des employés de services publics,* Canadian federation of government employees)

Louis Laberge, president of the FTQ (*Fédération des Travailleurs du Québec,* Quebec Federation of Labour)

Jean-Marc Kirouac, president of the UCC (*Union Catholique des Cultivateurs,* Catholic Farmers' Union)

Claude Ryan, editor of *Le Devoir*

Jacques Parizeau, president of the executive committee of the *Parti québecois*

Fernand Daoust, secretary of the *Parti québecois*

Yvon Charbonneau, president of the CEQ (*Corporation des Enseignants du Québec,* Quebec Teachers' Corporation)

Mathias Rioux, president of the *Alliance des professeurs de Montréal,* Montreal Teachers' Association

Camille Laurin, parliamentary leader of the *Parti québecois*

Guy Rocher, professor of sociology at the University of Montreal

Fernand Dumont, director of the *Institut supérieur des sciences humaines* (Institute of Humanities) at Laval University

Paul Bélanger, professor of political science at Laval University

Raymond Laliberté, ex-president of the CEQ

Marcel Rioux, professor of sociology at the University of Montreal

On the following day, October 15, the Canadian Army began to occupy Quebec, especially Montreal. Early in the morning of Friday, October 16, the government of Canada proclaimed a state of martial law under the War Measures Act, claiming that an insurrection was about to break out in Quebec. The federal government made it known through the newspapers that it had thus acted at the request of the government of Quebec and the municipal authorities of Montreal.

What Really Happened?

It is still too early to answer this question. Perhaps we will never know all the details of what happened, but we can still establish certain facts and make certain hypotheses.

From the beginning of the affair, Ottawa and Montreal clearly favoured a hard line: no negotiations with bandits and murderers. The Quebec government vacillated, and within it two different positions confronted each other. Choquette, the Minister of Justice, had become the leader of a minority of cabinet ministers, English-speaking or assimilated people, who supported Trudeau and Drapeau. Premier Bourassa, more inclined to negotiate, was playing for more time, but was forced to yield to pressures from all sides. Trudeau could rely on the Canadian Army to back up his point of view, and Drapeau had the Montreal police force, but Bourassa had only the Quebec Provincial Police, who were scattered throughout the province and were untrained for any large-scale manoeuvres.

Is it likely that the Premier of Quebec opened formal negotiations with the FLQ without the approval of Ottawa? Given the general climate and the special relationship between the two governments, one might infer that Ottawa assented to this move to give the army time to deploy its troops for the occupation of Quebec on Thursday of the same week. It has since come to light that there never was any real negotiation between the FLQ and Quebec, any more than there was negotiation with Ottawa. On Wednesday, Premier Bourassa told the editor of *Le Devoir*, Claude Ryan, that Quebec was going to restrict the terms of the negotiations. Endorsed by Trudeau and

Drapeau, the hard line was soon victorious. Bourassa had no choice but to give in to it.

Martial Law and Apprehended Insurrection

It was apparently decided to send the army to occupy Quebec shortly after the kidnapping of Laporte. Does anyone believe that an analysis of the forces then present in Quebec could suggest a possible insurrection? The government of Canada believed it, and so did the municipal government of Montreal, but up to now nobody has offered the slightest proof of the existence of this insurrection.

The FLQ never consisted of more than a few cells, a few dozen people at most. Such a group could hardly overthrow the government and establish their own regime in Quebec. To terrify the public, Mr. Marchand spoke of 3000 members of the FLQ.

The government of Canada maintains that several hundred sticks of dynamite and a quantity of arms had been stolen in Quebec. As of now (November 6, 1970), 116 offensive weapons and 2609 sticks of dynamite have been recovered. The police claim that there are 1800 more stolen dynamite sticks that have not yet been found. Did we really need a declaration of "war," the suspension of civil liberties, and a campaign of police raids unprecedented in Quebec's history, all to find these weapons and these dynamite sticks?

Since the proclamation of the War Measures Act, it has been stated that a parallel government was ready to assume power in Quebec and to act as an interim government pending a separatist take-over. This parallel government was supposedly made up of the personalities whose press release we have quoted above. Except for a few journalists hard up for copy, nobody believed this fantastic rumour. The press conference of the "personalities" was held on Wednesday at 9 p.m.; at that moment, the government of Canada had already begun to mobilize the troops. The "parallel government" cannot therefore explain the declaration of war and the occupation.

Why then did Ottawa react as it did? It clearly came as an unpleasant shock to Ottawa to realize that many people in Quebec were sympathetic to the FLQ. The federal government was alarmed at the number of individuals and groups that were urging the Quebec government to negotiate with the FLQ; it was also astonished by the fact that FRAP had broad popular support and was receiving help from several organizations and individuals in Montreal and in the province as a whole. This movement, described by Drapeau as a terrorist organization, was indirectly supported by a ministry of the Quebec government, by Montreal educational institutions and by the Catholic Church. One thing was certain: the general political climate of Quebec was not favourable enough to federalism and the status quo; the idea of independence was gaining too much ground. Trudeau's Minister of Propaganda, Jean Marchand, declared that every key sector of Quebec society had been infiltrated, that Quebec was ripe for revolution. Trudeau's Liberal team had been given a mandate to "put Quebec in its place" and above all to eliminate the idea of independence; it suddenly realized that things were not going very well in Quebec from this point of view.

For these reasons, the government of Canada decided to strike a hard blow against separatism. Tarring the FLQ, FRAP and the PQ with the same brush, it decided to have done with them all, and unleashed the police and military forces of Canada and Quebec.

At 5 a.m. on Friday, October 16, these forces began their offensive, arresting hundreds of citizens and conducting searches in the homes of thousands of others. These operations were carried out without a warrant and at any hour of the day or night. The police struck hard at the members of the *Parti québecois,* of FRAP and of all left-wing groups; in Quebec, they were arresting anything that moved. No reasons were given for the arrests and the detainees were not allowed to communicate with their lawyers for several days.

The Prime Minister of Canada declared a few days later that he had been elected to combat separatism and that he was attempting to live up to his mandate. His Minister of Propaganda, Marchand, stated in British Columbia, at the other end of Canada, that FRAP was a "cover" for the FLQ, thus insinuating that there was no difference between the terrorist FLQ and the democratic FRAP.

The Death of Laporte

On Saturday, October 17, the police found the body of the Quebec cabinet minister Pierre Laporte in the trunk of the car which had been used to abduct him. This death, which nobody had expected, raised the collective hysteria in Quebec to its highest pitch, and also admirably abetted the government of Canada. Because the FLQ had killed Laporte, it was therefore dangerous, and the government had therefore done the right thing to employ extraordinary measures and to arrest all those vicious leftists, separatists and protesters.

Canadian society felt itself menaced in the very depths of its being. The information media, which the federal government had accused of having too much to say before the occupation, quickly became the instrument of a government policy to create a climate of dismay, guilt and panic. The owners of these media became more than ever the firm advocates of the established order.

Every man in public life, at whatever level, had the right to a soldier for his personal bodyguard and to four soldiers for the protection of his residence. Public buildings and the offices of big companies also had the right to their own soldiers. Some of the powerful men in commerce and industry were also protected in this way. Power became visible and identifiable.

Information became more and more rare. Each

person thought it wise to go beyond the official censorship and impose self-censorship. Those who had been most in agreement with the government policy took a sweet revenge on their opponents of every stripe, denouncing the more notorious ones. How many thousands of people phoned the police to accuse the criminal of their choice? Persons known to be, or suspected of being, separatists or leftists were deluged by anonymous letters, threatening their lives. The conservative-minded regained control of the situation. This psychological bludgeoning of the population reached its high point in the funeral of Laporte. The population was informed of all the extraordinary security precautions that had been taken; the media broadcast a speech by the Prime Minister of Canada against terrorism, and with the evident intent of terrorizing the people himself, Trudeau adopted the tone and type of argumentation that the FLQ had used. It was "your little girl, Mádame, or the manager of your local bank" who were going to be the next victims. During the funeral the politicians were protected by soldiers with submachine guns trained on the crowd. For several hours, CBC television displayed a photograph of Laporte on the screen, accompanied by appropriate music. The psychological club was wielded with even more vigour in the areas of Quebec outside Montreal. The petty princes of the local information media had a field day: they lauded respect for the established order, Confederation, the encouragement of private enterprise. As the editorialist for a rural radio station so bluntly put it: "Recently, we have heard too much in Quebec about revolution, liberation and social justification. All that is finished now. We must support the government of Canada and do whatever we can to ensure the prosperity of private enterprise in Quebec." There was a man, at least, who had understood the message of the establishment.

Independence of Whom?

Several observers of the Quebec scene feel that independence is inevitable. People are now beginning to ask themselves: "Who will be the economic allies of a free Quebec?" In October 1970, an economist of the University of Montreal, Rodrigue Tremblay, published a pamphlet which is sure to provoke many debates. Tremblay advocates the political independence of Quebec and its economic association with the United States in a kind of Common Market. René Lévesque's *Parti québecois,* on the other hand, favours a common market between Quebec and Canada. The idea of independence is making progress, whatever the precise solutions offered.

The following passage from Tremblay's preface will give an idea of the tone of the work: "The participation of Quebec in a common market with Canada rather than with the United States would cost the citizens of Quebec a minimum of two billion dollars per year. Both I and other French-Canadian economists have made scientific analyses of the problem. With the highest degree of precision that is humanly possible under the circumstances, we can establish that, on the economic level at least, the participation of Quebec in a Canadian common market would be doubly disadvantageous to its citizens. *This type of common market, which we regard as contrary to nature, would do more than cost Quebec at least two billion dollars a year or 335 dollars per capita, through artificially high prices and an inefficient market structure;* it would also keep personal incomes at one of the lowest levels in North America. The incomes of Quebec residents as a whole (85 per cent French-speaking, 15 per cent English-speaking) are about 11 per cent below the Canadian average; they are 27 per cent below incomes in Ontario; 50 per cent below those in the United States as a whole; 75 per cent below those on the American West Coast. The position of the French-speaking Quebecker alone is even worse, because the English-speaking minority of Quebec receives, as a group, the highest incomes in Canada, a fact established by the Royal Commission on Bilingualism and Biculturalism. In Quebec, the mean personal income of French-speaking people is 35 per cent lower than that of English-speaking people."[14]

A former cabinet minister of the *Union Nationale* government, Mr. Beaulieu, has already publicly endorsed the idea of a common market with the United States. We would not be surprised to see other Quebec politicians adopt the same attitude in the near future. Has the *Parti québecois* not looked into this possibility because of some residue of sentimental feeling towards Canada?

Those separatists who dream of a new life in a different type of society are not reassured by the idea of a common market with the United States. Would such a market not greatly increase the influence on us of the American way of life — today so roundly condemned by American youth itself? Those separatist groups which want to build a socialist state must realize that a rapprochement to the United States would strengthen the capitalist system in Quebec. What would happen to the French language in a situation where the American influence was even greater? In the critical times in which we are living, these questions become more and more pertinent and more and more distressing.

And After?

October is behind us. The military occupation is to last until April 30, 1971, but the most shameful memories are already half-buried in the winter snows. In the course of this winter, we must strengthen our resolve and clarify our objectives, for Quebec has an appointment with destiny, make no mistake of that. The novelist Jacques Ferron has invited us to keep that rendezvous: "In my helplessness and loneliness, I listened to an old word, a word learned in school but up to then devoid of meaning and sonorously dull. This word came suddenly to life and rose up, echoing in the air which reverberated to the buzz of helicopters and the wail of sirens — the word 'Destiny'. . . Those days have taught me only two things: first of all, that the murmurs of destiny, though as preposterous as the whir of helicopter blades, made my ear more sensitive to the voice of the collective consciousness; secondly, that this return of an old and forgotten idea will help us to take our future more firmly in hand. In the end, the biter will be bit."[15]

The people of Quebec have already come to their senses; they are beginning to understand that the road to independence will be strewn with ever greater difficulties. An old and obstinate race, they know that if they want freedom, they must take it.

Chapter 11
Quebec in Transition

. . . Thus, entire peoples lose themselves,
Come to nothing, are not born . . .

Maurice Clavel

Let us use the metaphor of *social metabolism* to help us understand the rapid changes now occuring both in Quebec and in the rest of the world. Metabolism implies transformation: breakdown and reconstruction, death, birth and the struggle for birth. The metabolism of present-day societies is profoundly affected by a number of processes of breakdown and reconstruction. Some of these processes are peculiar to Quebec; others are common to all the industrial societies.

In an analysis of social metabolisms, the categories of *temporality* and *possibility* are of the utmost importance; this is especially true for Quebec. When we study the present state of Quebec society, we must pay particular attention to the *moments in time* when the processes of breakdown and reconstruction appear. To determine Quebec's future, we must examine the *possibilities*, bearing in mind that these possibilities will be determined by the moments at which developments in Quebec intersect with the evolutionary trends in western civilization as a whole.

Quebec is a society in transition: some of its ideas, values and institutions are declining and disappearing, while others are coming into being. Quebec, at a later stage in its development than most industrial societies, is undergoing the breakdown of both traditional culture and the colonial mentality. It is also subject to the processes of decomposition we find in overdeveloped economies everywhere. All of these tendencies are interacting, and they have made Quebec, to use our metaphor, a social metabolism in a feverish state. No wonder some people think Quebec society is dissolving before their very eyes!

Can Quebec Survive as a Nation?

The greatest challenge confronting Quebec today is survival—not as an administrative region dominated by the United States and Canada,[1] but as a nation. Culture is the key to this national survival. Any human group which, like the Québécois, is a distinct national entity and has its own social metabolism may be regarded as having a structure of symbols (culture) which shapes the structure of individuals and things. In other words, man's relationships to his environment and to other men are governed by a complex of values, attitudes and common modes of behaviour which give these relationshops meaning and constitute a culture. This culture controls the metabolism of society. In the words of François Meyer, a specialist in evolution: "These symbolic structures undoubtedly represent the analogue of the structures that ensure the survival of a species as an adaptive equilibrium . . . these structures govern the play of the economic, judicial and ethical exchanges, i.e. in the strict sense, the metabolism of the group."[2] Culture thus embodies and conditions political and economic phenomena; when it begins to erode, the human group supporting it is itself menaced with extinction.

The Québécois have, in the past, managed to preserve much of their culture because they lived in isolation on the fringes of a North American society different in lifestyle and mentality. But as they become more and more integrated into the mainstream of industrial society, can they survive as a people and a culture? Pierre Deffontaines, a French geographer who studied the effects of winter on Quebec society, put this dilemma rather well when, in 1957, he asked: are the Québécois in danger of losing their winter, having won it, having mastered it? This question still seems relevant and important twenty years later. Let us try to answer Deffontaines' question by examining the recent changes in Quebec culture and considering the possible alternatives for future action.

The Decline of Traditional Culture

By traditional culture in Quebec we mean Catholic religion, French, the parish, kith and kin, big families, docile workers. Since all of these characteristics are presently in decline, many of the most conservative Québécois believe that their culture itself is on the wane. They want to revive those specific cultural traits which have historically been the strong points of their society. It is understandable that these conservatives should pass from the smugness of yesteryear to the existential anxiety of today. The urban industrial lifestyle has appeared relatively late in Quebec. It has been imposed from without and attacked from within by the Quebec elites with their traditional ideology. Then, too, this new lifestyle coincides with the breakdown of the colonial mentality and with the aggravation of the contradictions apparent in all industrial societies.

These opponents of change are, however, confusing culture with its external manifestations. Culture is, as defined above, a complex of symbols embedded in a human group; and this culture can retain its integrity even when, as happens in periods of transition, the group abandons some concrete cultural traits in favour of others. The Québécois are giving up their religion, pursuing the delights of individualism, having smaller families, and, generally speaking, assuming the lifestyle common in urban industrial societies everywhere. But there still remains a distinctively Québécois way of perceiving and living in the world.

The Decline of the Colonial Mentality

The rapid rate of change in Quebec is partly due to the fact that the decline of the colonial mentality — which fosters the independence movement — occurs at the same time as the decline of the traditional culture. These two processes have not always been associated in the societies where they have arisen. In Quebec, however, they mutually reinforce one another. The widespread support for independence would hardly have been possible without significant changes in Quebec culture; and the decline of the colonial mentality, so deeply rooted in Quebec society, has contributed to cultural change by making a break with the past. In particular, the disappearance of the resignation, submission and docility associated with the colonial mentality has helped to change the Québécois' attitudes towards their political institutions, ruling elites and national history and has led them to introduce the ideas of liberty and self-determination into their personal lives.

These two declines of the colonial mentality and of the traditional culture, so characteristic of Quebec society today, have served to stimulate the social metabolism of Quebec, and have thereby produced a variety of transformations among the people of Quebec as a whole. Since both of these processes are gradual, the old and new coexist: we find both archaism and modernism in values and attitudes, the proportion of which varies with social class and group. This coexistence explains both the impatience of the conservatives who would like to restore the old order and the impatience of the innovators who call for a new society.

Changes for the Better

There are, fortunately, some changes for the better which correspond to the decline of the traditional culture and the colonial mentality. These changes cannot be evaluated in a quantitative way, like unemployment or GNP statistics; yet they are making a real contribution towards the creation of meaningful social relationships and a national identity.

Quebec, like other societies, possesses a strong life of the imagination: its individuals and communities have definite ideas of what is impossible, improbable, possible and certain in their lives. This collective imagination has undergone great changes in the last few years. May we not, with Hegel, think that this revolutionary change in the imaginative life of society will soon lead to a complete transformation of society itself?

Quebec's creative artists have done much in the past few years to reshape the imaginative life of their society. The creators of songs, poetry, theatre, cinema, music and the plastic and visual arts have helped the Québécois to obtain a better imaginative grasp of who they are and what their country is. In some cases, these artists have helped to bridge the generation gap and to reveal vital continuities on Quebec life. Pierre Perrault has made a film about one community in Quebec where people were working to revive their culture.[3] People everywhere are asking questions about how they live now and are working to create a new Quebec society whose outlines they have begun to grasp.

In fact, the idea of a new Quebec society has caught on not just among artists, but among Québécois at large. Even politicians whose class interests favour dependence find themselves obliged to pay lip service to the idea of a revived national life.[4] Some of the most significant steps in the revival of Quebec's culture have been taken by ordinary people in their city districts, neighbourhoods, factories and workplaces. People have been working together to create ties of solidarity that foster real human relationships and identity. At Saint-Jérome, at Longueuil, in the Gaspé region, in the Montreal neighbourhoods and elsewhere, communities are becoming more and more aware of their exploitation and alienation and are beginning to realize that they themselves should be primarily responsible for their own lives. This is a form of cultural sovereignty which the establishment finds hard to accept.

Quebec's Future in the Global Village

The Québécois who want to create a new society may take heart at the cultural developments of recent years. With the impetus provided by the Quiet Revolution, they seem to have shaken off a centuries-old conditioning that resulted from the colonization and domination of their country; and they seem to be capable of finding within themselves the resources necessary to create a new blueprint for society, which can be realized through independence. The Québécois cannot, like their ancestors in the nineteenth century, respond to threats of assimilation by passive resistance, by withdrawal into themselves. They are part of the global village, and their options will be determined by the future course of events in the world at large.

Let us consider two widespread and fundamentally contradictory visions of the shape of things to come on this planet. In one vision, unrestrained economic growth and its associated technological development should continue indefinitely into the future. The multinationals are the prime movers in a continuing economic exploitation which reduces the ordinary man to a passive consumer and destroys both our national and our human resources. In this view of things, Quebec becomes a distant suburb of the American industrial centres. The steamroller of American imperialism flattens Quebec as it has flattened Canada, and Quebec's culture disintegrates. In such circumstances, the Québécois become one of those peoples who, in the words of Maurice Clavel, "lose themselves, come to nothing, are not born."

In the second vision, mankind is entering a period of transition towards a major new stage in social evolution. This view of the world's future has emerged from the work of biologists, ecologists, economists and sociologists in several countries. Most of these experts believe that, if we all use what we now know about ourselves and our environment, we can get through this transition period successfully. This moment in the world's social evolution is, however, a time of great crisis. In his study of world demographic and technological growth curves, which he regards as more than exponential, François Meyer concludes that we will soon face a situation of extreme emergency: the acceleration of growth, which has increased steadily over the last few millenia, will suddenly give way to a drastic downturn in all the curves. According to Meyer, the accelerated rate of change is already breaking down the traditional economic, political, ethical, religious and cultural structures of human society.[5]

In the face of this world crisis, the experts are beginning to suggest that we must adopt a different kind of economic development. Essentially, the economic development of the future will have to be decentralized; in other words, the national communities must be self-managed and in control of the economic life of their own territories. Even conservative politicians like France's President Giscard are beginning to advocate this new type of economic development.

Quebec, like many societies around the world, finds itself at a crossroads. On one hand, the Québécois may continue to accept an economic system based on the exploitation of man and nature, a system which has destroyed our humanity, our symbols, our human relationships and our identity. They may acquiesce in a world order dominated by multinationals like ITT, General Motors and Royal Dutch Shell. The great poet Pablo Neruda has described the plight of his native Chile under such a regime:

When the trumpets sounded,
All was ready on earth,
And Jehovah divided the world
among Coca-Cola Inc., Anaconda,
Ford Motors,
and a few other corporations;
The United Fruit Co.
Reserved the juiciest part for itself,
The central coast of my land,
The sweet girdle of America.

There is no one such privileged corporation in Quebec. Because Quebec is an internal colony of Canada and Canada is the biggest colony of the United States, the Québécois are exploited by a host of multinationals.

But if the Québécois are prepared to study the current developments in industrial civilization as a whole, they may decide to exercise their freedom of choice. They may make up their minds to preserve what has accumulated here in Quebec in the way of human relationships, collective memory and identity. If the people of Quebec decide that they want to come to something, to be born as a nation, they may be able to preserve their heritage and rediscover a society with a human face.

Chapter 12
The End of Innocence?

Quebec has been an issue in Canadian politics since the Conquest, but the question of its status did not become critical until the 1960s. At that time, both internal and external pressures made people conscious of Quebec's political and economic dependence. Public opinion campaigns, movements and political parties emerged which favoured independence for Quebec and challenged the existing socioeconomic system. Founded in 1968, the *Parti québécois* offered a social democratic program of political sovereignty and socioeconomic reform and spearheaded a broad opposition movement to remove the moneymen from power and replace them with a national government. Since the victory of this party on November 15, 1976, the Québécois have been concerned not only with challenging the powers of Canada but with exercising the powers of Quebec under particularly difficult conditions. Let us see what forces are at play and what goals are at stake now that the rules of the game have changed.

The analysts have their way of interpreting the recent events in Quebec; but the day-to-day experience of the people is something quite different. Sometimes nothing seems to be happening; then, suddenly, change is everywhere. There is an alternation between the event and the process. The event is spectacular and easy to recognize; the process operates over a longer period of time and is more hidden, more underground. Though the two are related, the process does not completely explain the event, nor does the event reveal all the processes at work in a society at a given moment.[1] The October crisis of 1970, the public service employees' strike in the fall of 1972 and the Liberal victory of 1973 were events which seemed to leave Quebec with no resolution of its contradictions and confrontations. Then the *Parti québécois* was elected. The rules of the game changed — to the displeasure of the media men with their ready-made formulas—and the conflicts and contradictions grew more acute. All this should remind us of Marx's image of the underground labour of the mole.

The election of the *Parti québécois* has completely altered the situation in Quebec, revealing processes already at work and giving rise to others. This event (or advent) did not meet with as draconian a response as the crises of 1970 and 1972. During the FLQ crisis, the federal government sent in the troops, and order reigned in Quebec. During the strike of the public service employees, the federal government's henchmen in the province imprisoned the union leaders, and order reigned once more. Each time, the members of the ruling class hoped that the problem had been solved and that the protesters of every conviction had been put down once and for all. As a rule, the members of the ruling elite are fond of concealing their power, and on occasion they even pose as victims of the dominated class. Though they were forced to reveal themselves in 1970 and 1972, they did not seem to realize that the Québécois had come to know them for what they were and were familiar with the agencies and instruments of violence through which they exercised their power. The brutal object lessons of 1970 and 1972 have not been lost on the citizens of Quebec, especially the workers, and these lessons have helped to nourish their reformism and their radicalism.

When the *Parti québécois* was elected in November 1976, the federal government could not use the tactics it had employed in 1970 and 1972. It had to respect the rules of parliamentary democracy; it could neither send in the troops nor imprison the leaders of the independence movement. The ruling class resorted to a more subtle and insidious form of violence, an economic terrorism distilled drop by drop. It now waged war through hostages and agents provocateurs, and made veiled attempts to undermine the little power that the *Parti québécois* had managed to take from it.

Absolute ends and responsibility

A German sociologist, Max Weber, can help us to understand how attitudes have changed in Quebec since the election of the *Parti québécois*. Weber makes a useful distinction between two kinds of ethical systems. The first, which he calls the ethic of absolute ends, is based on moral values and considers only the quality of an act itself. The second system, which he calls the ethic of responsibility, judges an act in the light of its consequences and takes actual results into consideration.[2] The Québécois are now abandoning the ethic of absolute ends in favour of the ethic of responsibility. This passage from one ethical system to the other is what can be termed the end of innocence in Quebec.

For many years, people who opposed Quebec's political dependence and economic exploitation were chiefly inspired by moral values; in Weber's terms, they followed the ethic of absolute ends. When the *Parti québécois* was elected, many opponents of the system found themselves no longer in the street but in the National Assembly. With the acquisition of power, the elected representatives of the *Parti québécois* and their supporters had to turn to the ethic of responsibility to discover ways to implement the values and goals they had adopted earlier under the ethic of absolute ends. In these new circumstances, the Québécois have had to give up their absolute moral certitude and the naiveté and candour that accompanies it. They have discovered that they are not alone in the world and that this world is neither as idealistic nor as disinterested as they had imagined.

The Québécois now realize that their own masters are part of a network of ruling classes and dominant states which controls the entire planet. This world-wide elite is disturbed by any attempt to change the status quo anywhere, and it is not surprising that Russian officials — the only Russians who may express an opinion — are not in favour of independence for Quebec.[3] This of course does not mean that the Chinese support the idea. In the past, the

Québécois were isolated from the world and lived in a state of innocence. They are losing that innocence as they move out into the world and discover that the logic of domination knows no frontiers. They are beginning to understand that, in international politics as in their own daily lives, the ethic of responsibility overcomes the ethic of absolute ends.

Obstacles

The *Parti québécois* is encountering a number of obstacles in its way, among them the Canadian ruling class. The United States power elite has apparently deputized its Canadian counterpart to discredit the reform movement in Quebec and maintain the status quo in the northern part of the continent. The ruling class in the United States dominates the Americas, and the *Parti québécois* represents a threat (however slight) to that domination. In particular, the American elite is worried about the social blueprint which the *Parti québécois* drew up in the years before its election, because this program features social democracy as well as independence Both the American and Canadian elites, who work hand in glove and share the same interests, have a greater fear of socialism, even of the democratic kind, than of Quebec independence. Relying on this ideological bond and on the common culture in Canada and the United States, the Americans have adopted an official hands-off policy towards Quebec: they prefer to leave it to the Canadians to solve the problem.

The *Parti québécois* must deal with other problems within Quebec itself. It has undertaken a complete overhaul of society, and such an upheaval usually blurs the outlines of the class struggle. Confused by the shifting play of economic, social and political forces, people often fail to realize where their best interests lie and to appreciate what the party is trying to do for them. Then, too, the *Parti québécois* must deal with the range of problems afflicting all industrialized countries today: unemployment, inflation, energy and environmental crises. In this daily struggle, the conflicts and confrontations multiply and may, in the long run, threaten the government itself.

There is also a danger that the pressures of these multiple tasks, especially winning political sovereignty, will force the *Parti québécois* to compromise its program of social democratic reform. Since the early 1960s, when the Quiet Revolution gave birth to new social movements, a number of Québécois have favoured independence only because they could look beyond it to the establishment of a new type of society based on principles of social and economic democracy. They also believed that the majority of their countrymen would eventually welcome such a society. These social democrats welcome the fact that the *Parti québécois* has adopted policies embodying much of their ideology. But given the ambiguities of the present political situation, they are beginning to wonder whether the *Parti québécois* will be able to achieve its social democratic goals.

The current preoccupation with Quebec's political status, which shows no signs of diminishing in the future, is definitely harmful to the *Parti québécois* program of social reform. The business interests who dominate the economy of Quebec are well aware that their position is secured by legal and constitutional provisions. They want to avoid any change in these arrangements which might threaten their dominant position; and this naturally explains their concern for constitutional issues. On the other hand, to achieve far-reaching socioeconomic reforms, the *Parti québécois* has to acquire much greater political autonomy. But at the same time it must proclaim "business as usual" to reassure the companies and individuals who fear for their livelihoods and savings. This terrible dilemma is probably the greatest obstacle to the creation of social democracy in Quebec. The *Parti québécois* is constantly threatened by economic destabilization; but if it yields to the forces of capitalism and imperialism and puts off its socioeconomic reforms to engage in constitutional disputes, it will almost certainly be defeated at the polls.

Despite the many obstacles in their path, we need not conclude that the Québécois are doomed. In the last fifteen years, they have called into question many of their institutions, values and ideas. Through a series of confrontations, they have come to realize that their problems are largely caused by political and economic domination. Today, most Québécois reject a piecemeal approach to their problems: they want to study all aspects of their domination and to understand how it has affected their lives as a whole. They may take comfort in the thought that it may be relatively easy to restructure a close-knit society like their own. But they must face up to the fact that in North America they are the only group of any importance that wants to change the established order.[4]

Quebec and the Constitution

Poorly informed and constantly reassured by their masters, Canadians were ill-prepared for the election of the *Parti québécois*. But faced with what they regarded as a threat to their country, they soon began to ask themselves questions not only about Quebec but also about Canada. Divergent interests and viewpoints have emerged in different regions and provinces, along with critical remarks about the political organization of Canada.

Today, people are beginning to criticize and to call into question the British North America Act, which only yesterday seemed a universal model of government. Many people are calling for its revision. Though some Canadians have already travelled a long way on the road to constitutional reform, it will be a long time before fruitful negotiations can begin between Canada and Quebec. People in this country are slow to tamper with their political arrangements, as one can judge by the time it took the Québécois to reject political and economic dependence.

To date, the Canadians who seem most ready to deal with the grievances of Quebec recognize that there must be constitutional guarantees to assure Quebec's linguistic and cultural security. This is not surprising: Mr. Trudeau's policy of institutional bilingualism and the promulgation of the French-language charter in Quebec have focused attention on language and culture. The Canadians who have gone furthest along the road of compromise would seem to have arrived at approximately the position of Mr. Bourassa and at something which would resemble his nebulous "cultural sovereignty". This position is unfortunately several years behind the development of ideas in Quebec, particularly those which form the basis for the program and ideology of the *Parti québécois*.

The central issue here is the relationship between language and culture on the one hand and politics and economics on the other. To speak of cultural sovereignty in a politically and economically dependent state is to pretend, with Mr. Bourassa, that sovereignty is divisible and that no relationship exists between these different aspects of life. But both theory and practice show that they are closely linked and influence each other. Most Québécois speak an endangered language because they have always been dominated and have not been in control of their economic life.[5] To remedy the effects of over two hundred years of dependence, the government of Quebec must change the overall situation by acquiring political sovereignty. We would soon realize the need for political sovereignty if the majority of Québécois decided that they wanted to create a new social order. We cannot transform our political and economic life as long as it is controlled by foreigners, nor can we develop new values and a new culture if they collide with the political and economic values of the surrounding imperialistic powers. Every dominated society encounters these fundamental problems, and Quebec is no exception. Patching up the BNA Act is certainly no solution.

Two Nationalisms in Confrontation?

For years people have talked a great deal about

French-Canadian nationalism and, more recently, about Québécois nationalism. It's the villain in the Canadian tragi-comedy: "Put the donkey on trial!" is the cry.[6] There has recently been talk of a Canadian nationalism born in reaction to both American imperialism and, even more, to Québécois nationalism. This is an opposition movement of an entirely new and aberrant type: a state nationalism! Some years ago Prime Minister Trudeau wrote: "One of the ways of counterbalancing the appeal of separatism is to use time, energy and enormous amounts of money in the service of *federal* nationalism."[7] Mr. Trudeau, who does not readily let go of an idea, is now vigorously pursuing this policy and obtaining good results. In Canada he is stirring up "federal nationalism" and, in Quebec, he is giving powerful assistance to Quebec nationalism. To nourish two nationalisms is an impressive activity for a thinker as viscerally anti-nationalist as Mr. Trudeau.

Canada and Quebec are two nations, one federal, the other *human*. Since confrontations and negotiations may develop between these two forms of nationalism, we should consider whether this is a good or a bad thing. Paradoxically, Mr. Trudeau takes the same approach, in his thoughts and actions, as the *Parti québécois*. After its election on November 15, 1976, the *Parti québécois* remained true to the "sovereignty/association" formula it had adopted at its foundation in 1968. This formula advocates that once the two national entities are recognized as such, "supranational" institutions should be created to assure both economic cooperation and the development of each according to its particular nature. This approach suggests that economic union and cultural sovereignty should go hand in hand and that Quebec should only seek independence as a last resort if Canada were to refuse economic collaboration on the European Common Market model. This seems to be the major policy position of the *Parti québécois*, and we may hope that the two nations have enough creative imagination to discover the kinds of association which would allow both Canadians and Québécois to develop freely.

Between the Past and the Future

Let us ask the final question about Quebec: is the game worth the candle? Quebec has become more and more of a problem in the last few years; is it worth the expenditure of so much energy, resources and money? The modernists agree that the Québécois have already liberated themselves from the institutions, ideas and values which kept them from progressing like their American and Canadian cousins. The realistic federalists admit that the Québécois, in rousing themselves to action and in challenging the confederal order, have uncovered a fine example of "regional economic disparity" which deserves to be remedied. The conservatives both in Canada and Quebec, who believe in preserving cultural heritages, are prepared to recognize that Quebec's language and culture is endangered and must be protected by statute. All these people think that the game is worth the candle as long as we stop short of destroying national unity. In the present circumstances, we are sacrificing far too much to this sacred cow of national unity. What can "national unity" mean when there are two nations in confrontation, both of which want to survive and flourish? Does it mean that Quebec should continue to be dominated, as it has been for centuries?

Even those who believe that the Québécois are right to rebel base their views more on the past and the present than on the future. They share the dominant North American idea that evolution has finally produced on this continent a type of society towards which all other people should strive. In this view, politics is a matter of making slight changes in the established order and of leaving it to the large corporations and multinationals to organize the entire earth and its peoples. It takes for granted that brutal economic growth will continue indefinitely, destroying our human and natural resources.

The Québécois, however, are now more concerned with the quality of life and society than with constitutional quibbles, the growth of the GNP or even political nationalism. Their daily life reflects this concern, which represents a challenge to the North American model of society. Realists may say that the Québécois do not have the strength for such utopian social reconstruction, but no one will deny that from this perspective the game is amply worth the candle. Perhaps, after all, Quebec has not yet come to the very end of innocence.

Footnotes

1: The Quebec Question

1. Jacques Berque, " 'Contenu' et 'Forme' dans la décolonisation," in *Perspectives de la Sociologie contemporaine*. Paris: Presses universitaires de France, 1968, p. 30.
2. Arnold J. Toynbee, *Civilization on Trial*. New York: Oxford University Press, 1948, p. 161.
3. Marcel Rioux and Robert Sévigny, *Les Nouveaux citoyens, enquête sociologique sur les jeunes du Québec*. Radio-Canada Montréal, 1965. This enquiry covered a sampling of 806 young Quebeckers (boys and girls) from 18 to 21, selected from all regions of the country.

2: From Frenchmen to Habitants

1. Georges Langlois, *Histoire de la population canadienne-française*. Montreal: Éditions Albert Lévesque, 1934, p. 47.
2. Léon Gérin, *Aux sources de notre histoire*. Montreal: Fides, 1946, p. 256.
3. Robert Redfield, *Peasant Society and Culture*. Chicago: University of Chicago Press, 1956, p. 70.
4. Jacques Henripin, *La Population canadienne au début du XVIIIe siècle*. Paris: Presses universitaires de France, 1954, p. 3.
5. *Ibid.*, p. 3.
6. Max Derruau, *A l'origine du rang canadien. Cahiers de Géographie de Québec,* Presses universitaires Laval, nouv. série, I, October, 1956, p. 39.
7. Jean-Charles Falardeau, *Paroisses de France et de Nouvelle-France au XVIIe siècle, Cahiers de l'Ecole des Sciences Sociales, Politiques et Economiques de Laval,* vol. II, no. 7, 1943, pp. 9-10.
8. *Ibid.*, pp. 11-12.
9. *Ibid.*, pp. 14-15.
10. *Ibid.*, p. 18.
11. Léon Gérin, *L'Habitant de Saint-Justin. Proceedings and Transactions of the Royal Society of Canada,* second series, vol. 4, 1898, p. 204.
12. Falardeau, *op. cit.*, p. 24.
13. Gustave Lanctôt, *L'Administration de la Nouvelle-France.* Paris: H. Champion, 1929, p. 140.
14. Falardeau, *op. cit.*, pp. 24-25.

15. *Ibid.,* p. 25.

16. Joseph-Edmond Roy, *Histoire de la seigneurie de Lauzon.* Lévis: Mercier & Cie., 1898, vol. II, p. 63.

17. Léon Gérin, *Le Type économique et social des Canadiens.* Montreal: Fides, 1948, pp. 103-104.

18. Falardeau, *op. cit.,* p. 35.

19. Léon Gérin, *Monographie du Canada, l'Histoire de la Colonisation. Science Sociale,* Paris, 1894, vol. XVIII, pp. 337-338.

20. Falardeau, *op. cit.,* p. 37.

21. Francis Parkman, *France and England in North America, Part IV: The Old Régime in Canada.* Toronto: George N. Morang, 1898, p. 467.

22. Mason Wade, *The French Canadians: 1760-1967.* Toronto: Macmillan of Canada, 1968, vol. I, p. 6.

23. Quoted by Wade, *op. cit.,* p. 23.

24. Quoted by Wade, *op. cit.,* p. 23.

25. Quoted by Wade, *op. cit.,* p. 41.

26. Quoted by Wade, *op. cit.,* p. 42.

27. Quoted by Wade, *op. cit.,* p. 42.

28. Clément Brown, *L'Eveil de la nationalité canadienne-française* thesis in MS, Laval University; p. 145.

29. Quoted by Wade, *op. cit.,* p. 43.

30. Frances Brooke, *The History of Emily Montague* (orig. pub. 1769). Toronto: McClelland and Stewart Ltd., 1961, p. 167.

31. *Ibid.,* p. 117.

3: The defeated keep the faith

1. Translator's note. In one of his letters to Charles Augustin Feriol, comte d'Argental (no. 11488 in *Voltaire's Correspondence,* ed. Theodore Besterman, vol. LVII; *Institut et musée Voltaire, Les Délices,* Geneva, 1960), Voltaire spoke of some minor trouble his friend had gotten into that could be easily explained, but which had caused quite an uproar. He wrote: *"Voilà une grande tracasserie pour un mince sujet. Cela ressemble à la guerre des Anglais qui commença pour quatre arpents de neige . . ."* (What a big fuss over a little thing. It's like the war with the English, which started over four acres of snow . . .) This slighting definition of Canada has been corrupted to *quelques arpents de neige.*

2. Alfred Dubuc, *Les Classes sociales au Canada de 1760 à 1840,* mimeographed, University of Montreal, undated, p. 21.

3. Michel Brunet, *Premières réactions des vaincus de 1760 devant leurs vainqueurs. Revue d'histoire de l'Amérique française,* Institut d'histoire de l'Amérique française, Montreal, vol. VI, no. 4, 1953, pp. 506-516.

4. Guy Frégault, *La Guerre de la conquête*. Montreal: Fides, 1955, p. 455.

5. Michel Brunet, "La Conquête anglaise et la déchéance de la bourgeoisie canadienne, 1760-1793," *Amérique française*, XII, 2, June 1955, p. 27. All the following Brunet quotations are from the same work.

6. Louis-F. G. Baby, "L'exode des classes dirigeantes à la cession du Canada," *The Canadian Antiquarian and Numismatic Journal*, third series, 2, 1899, p. 118.

7. Brunet, *op. cit.*, p. 29. The word *bourgeoisie*, in socialist terminology, refers to the ruling class in a mercantile or industrial society.

8. *Ibid.*, p. 56.

9. Wade, *op. cit.*, p. 50.

10. Brunet, *op. cit.*, pp. 57-58.

11. *Ibid.*, pp. 71-72.

12. Auguste Viatte, *Histoire littéraire de l'Amérique française*. Quebec: Presses Universitaires Laval, 1954, pp. 47-48.

13. Brunet, *op. cit.*, p. 46.

14. Jean-Marc Léger, "Le Canada français à la recherche de son son avenir," *Esprit*, August-September, 1952, p. 260.

15. Jacques Henripin, "From Acceptance of Nature to Control," *The Canadian Journal of Economics and Political Science*, vol. 23, no. 1, 1957, pp. 13 and 15.

16. Henri Marrou, "Préface française," *Esprit*, August-September, 1952, p. 172, note 1.

17. Viatte, *op. cit.*, pp. 47-48.

18. Joseph-Edmond Roy, *op. cit.*, p. 194.

19. Wade, *op. cit.*, p. 86.

20. Wade, *op. cit.*, p. 102.

21. Frank Scott, "Canada et Canada français," *Esprit*, August-September, 1952, p. 185.

22. See especially Pierre-Elliott Trudeau, "Some Obstacles to Democracy in Quebec," in *Federalism and the French Canadians*. Toronto: McClelland & Stewart, 1967, pp. 103-123.

22. René Gillouin, *Aristarchie*. Geneva: Editions du Cheval ailé, 1946, pp. 28-33.

24. Wade, *op. cit.*, p. 109.

25. Quoted by Wade, *op. cit.*, pp. 109-110.

26. Wade, *op. cit.*, p. 117.

27. *Ibid.*, p. 118.

28. *Ibid.*, p. 119.

29. Marcel Trudel, *Le Régime seigneurial*, Canadian Historical Association. Historical booklet no. 6, Ottawa, 1956, p. 17.

30. Lionel Groulx, *Histoire du Canada français depuis la*

découverte. Montreal: Fides, 1960, vol. 2, p. 99.

31. *Ibid.,* p. 107.

32. Alfred Dubuc, *Les classes sociales au Canada de 1760 à 1840,* mimeographed course, *id.,* M., pp. 19-20, 1967.

33. Groulx, *op. cit.,* p. 131.

34. Fernand Ouellet, *Histoire économique et sociale du Québec: 1760-1850.* Montreal: Fides, 1966, pp. 421-22.

35. Groulx, *op. cit.,* p. 160.

36. Fernand Ouellet, *Les insurrections de 1837-1838: un phénomène social,* in *Histoire sociale,* no. 2, Ottawa, p. 54.

37. Fernand Ouellet, *Papineau dans la Révolution de 1837-1838,* Canadian Historical Association. Report of the Annual Meeting held at Edmonton, June 4-7, 1958, p. 20.

38. Groulx, *op. cit.,* pp. 163-164.

39. *Ibid.,* p. 163.

40. Ouellet, *op. cit.,* p. 73.

41. *Ibid.,* p. 81.

42. *Ibid.,* p. 66.

43. Quoted by Ouellet, *Histoire économique et sociale du Québec: 1760-1850,* p. 412.

44. *Ibid.,* p. 195.

45. *Ibid.,* p. 302.

46. *Ibid.,* p. 67.

47. Ouellet, *Les insurrections de 1837-1838,* p. 72.

48. Quoted by Gérard Filteau, *Histoire des Patriotes.* Montreal: Editions modèles, 1942, vol. 3, p. 243.

49. Fernand Dumont, "Idéologie et conscience historique dans la société canadienne-française au XIXe siècle," MS., 1965, p. 18.

50. Rapport de l'archiviste de la province du Québec, 1924-1925, facsimile.

4: The quiet conservatism of a colonized people

1. Wade, *op. cit.,* p. 186.

2. *Ibid.,* p. 197.

3. *Ibid.,* p. 208.

4. *Ibid.,* p. 212.

5. Quoted in *Histoire 1534-1968,* ed. D. Vaugeois and J. Lacoursière. Montreal: Editions du renouveau pédagogique, 1968, p. 329.

6. Quoted by Wade, *op. cit.,* pp. 253 and 252.

7. Dumont, *op. cit.,* p. 21.

8. Wade, *op. cit.,* p. 342.

9. Louvigny de Montigny, *Antoine Gérin-Lajoie.* Toronto: Ryerson Press, 1925, p. 13.

10. Michel Brunet, *Trois dominantes de la pensée canadienne-française. Ecrits du Canada français*, III, Montreal, 1957, pp. 98-100.

11. François-Xavier Garneau, *Histoire du Canada depuis sa découverte jusqu'à nos jours*. Quebec: N. Aubin, 1852, pp. 401-402.

12. Léon Pouliot, *La Réaction Catholique de Montréal, 1840-1841*. Montreal: Imprimerie du Messager, 1942.

13. Viatte, *op. cit.*, pp. 95 and 98.

14. Dumont, *op. cit.*, p. 13.

15. Viatte, *op. cit.*, p. 99.

16. Mgr. J. S. Raymond, "Enseignements des événements contemporains," *La Revue canadienne*, January, 1871, p. 38.

17. Thomas Chapais, *Discours et conférences*. Quebec: 1908, p. 39.

18. Louis Maheu has devoted his Master's thesis to the study of the problem, in the Department of Sociology, University of Montreal, 1966.

19. Viatte, *op. cit.*, p. 133.

20. Gérald Fortin, *An Analysis of the Ideology of a French-Canadian Nationalist Magazine, 1917-1953*, MS., Cornell University, 1956.

21. *Ibid.*, p. 205.

22. A. Faucher and M. Lamontagne, *French-Canadian Society*, vol. 1, ed. M. Rioux and Y. Martin. Toronto: McClelland & Stewart, 1964, p. 267.

23. Nathan Keyfitz, "Population Problems," in *French-Canadian Society*, vol. 1, ed. M. Rioux and Y. Martin. Toronto: McClelland & Stewart, 1964, p. 227.

24. Translator's note. Epinal is a city in France famous for the production of *images*, inexpensive and often poorly executed prints on a variety of popular themes. In the late eighteenth and early nineteenth centuries the images of Epinal were especially popular, and included a famous series on the various uniforms, regiments, etc., of the Napoleonic army. *Images d'Epinal* became a proverbial expression for a simple-minded outlook on life.

25. D. Vaugeois and J. Lacoursière, *op. cit.*, p. 540.

26. Maurice Tremblay, *La Pensée social au Canada français*, MS., 1950, pp. 33 and 36.

5: The springtime of Quebec

1. D. Vaugeois and J. Lacoursière, *op. cit.*, p. 539.

6: Liberty vs. the dollar

1. Maurice Séguin, *L'Idée de l'indépendance au Québec*. Trois-Rivières: Editions Boréal-Express, 1968.
2. André d'Allemagne, *Le colonialisme au Québec*. Montreal: Les Editions R-B, 1966.
3. I borrow these headings from André d'Allemagne.
4. D'Allemagne, *op. cit.*, p. 31.
5. *Ibid.*, p. 33.
6. Charles Bettelheim, *Planification et croissance accélérée.* Paris: Maspéro, 1967, p. 42.
7. *Fédération canadienne des employés de services publics.*
8. D'Allemagne, *op. cit.*, p. 67.
9. *Ibid.*, p. 85.
10. *Ibid.*, p. 88.
11. *Ibid.*, p. 86.
12. Quoted by Alain Bosquet, *Poésie du Québec*. Paris: Seghers, 1968, p. 26.
13. Paul Chamberland, in *Les Québecois*. Paris: Maspéro, 1967, p. 91. This whole anthology is worth reading.
14. D'Allemagne, *op. cit.*, p. 89.
15. *La Presse,* October 22, 1968.

7: The right of the richer

1. Clément-Charles Sabrevois de Bleury, *Réfutation de l'écrit de Louis-Joseph Papineau, ex-orateur de la chambre de l'assemblée du Bas-Canada, intitulé Histoire de l'insurrection du Canada, publié dans le recueil hebdomadaire, La Revue du progrès, imprimée à Paris*. Montreal: Imprimerie de J. Lovell, 1839, p. 54.
2. Pierre-Elliott Trudeau, *Federalism and the French Canadians*. Toronto: Macmillan, 1968.
3. *Ibid.*, from "Preface to the French Edition" by Gérard Pelletier, p. xvi.
4. *Ibid.*, pp. xxii-xxiii.
5. *Ibid.*, p. xxiii.
6. *Ibid.*, p. xxiii.
7. *Ibid.*, p. 196.
8. *Ibid.*, p. 197.
9. Chamberland, *op. cit.*, p. 83, note 4.
10. Lucio Magri, "L'Etat et la Révolution aujourd'hui," *Les Temps Modernes,* nos. 266-267, August-September, 1968, pp. 399-400, Paris.
11. Quoted by Trudeau, *op. cit.*, p. 181.
12. Henry Pratt Fairchild, ed., *Dictionary of Sociology.*

Totowa, N. J.: Littlefield, Adams & Co., 1965.
13. Trudeau, *op. cit.*, p. 3.
14. These figures, and the following ones, are taken from the excellent study by Richard Arès, S.J., "Un siècle de vie française en dehors du Québec," Revue d'histoire de l'Amérique française, vol. 21, no. 3a, numéro special, "Cent ans d'histoire 1867-1967," Montreal, 1967, pp. 533-570.
15. Trudeau, *op. cit.*, p. 139, note 10.
16. *Ibid.*, p. 193.
17. D'Allemagne, *op. cit.*, p. 14.

8: Quebec or French Canada?

1. This information is quoted from a report submitted by students as part of their term work.
2. Marcel Chaput, in *Le Journal de Montréal*, September 5, 1968.
3. *Le Devoir,* June 14, 1968.
4. *La Presse,* September 2, 1968.
5. *Le Devoir,* September 4, 1968.
6. Translator's note. The expression refers to the pronunciation of the word *cheval* by people careless of their speech. The term appears to have been invented by André Laurendeau, writing under the pseudonym Candide, in a *Le Devoir* article of October 21, 1959, entitled *La langue que nous parlons,* to refer to the shoddy, impoverished, and often ungrammatical type of French spoken by many people in Quebec.
7. *Le Devoir,* June 30, 1967.

9: Towards a free Quebec?

1. Translator's note. The incident is from "La chèvre de M. Seguin" by Alphonse Daudet, which appeared in *Lettres de mon Moulin* in 1866. The story was addressed to the poet Pierre Gringoire, a friend of Daudet's, who had turned down the offer of a good job on a Paris newspaper. Daudet wrote him this cautionary tale on the dangers of being too independent. In Daudet's words, "You will see what you get for wanting to live in freedom." In the story, M. Seguin loses goats who break their halter and go off to the mountains, where the wolf eats them. Having lost six goats, M. Seguin warns the seventh, Blanquette, about the wolf, but in vain. She goes to the mountain, eventually meets the wolf after one glorious day of freedom, and after an entire night of fending him off, she gives in at daybreak and lets herself be eaten.
2. Translator's note. *Franglais* is a word used to describe an

QUEBEC IN QUESTION/ 207

impure French that has been contaminated by a very large number of English words and expressions.

3. Translator's note. The author is here referring to a number of ideas derived from the Theory of Evolution. Biologists have noted that at certain times an underdeveloped or unspecialized species has had a better chance for survival than a more "evolved" or adapted species, due to a change of environment. Thus dinosaurs perished with the coming of an ice age, while weaker and less "adapted" but more adaptable species survived. Trotsky, in writing of the development of socialist societies, speaks of the "privilege of historical backwardness," or underdevelopment, enjoyed by societies at a low level of social evolution; such societies had the opportunity of omitting the *bourgeois* stage in Marx's scheme of historical evolution (tribal communism — slave societies — feudalism — capitalism — revolution — socialism) and going directly from, say, feudalism to communism. Thorstein Veblen used an hypothesis he called "the law of combined development" to explain the extremely rapid advance of Germany as an industrial and political power in the nineteenth century. Here, too, Germany seems to have benefitted from being "behind" England and France in terms of the evolution of its society. Professor Rioux is here wondering whether the same evolutionary "privileges" will be enjoyed by Quebec.

For a discussion of the application of the Theory of Evolution to human societies, see especially Thomas G. Harding et al., *Evolution and Culture,* ed. Marshall D. Sahlins and Elman R. Service. Ann Arbor: University of Michigan Press, 1960.

4. Michel Brunet, *Québec, Canada anglais.* Montreal: Editions HMH Ltée, 1967, pp. 91-92.

5. Important figure in the British Empire and mentor of Mr. Trudeau, the Prime Minister of Canada.

6. D'Allemagne, *op. cit.,* p. 64.

7. Fernand Dumont, "La représentation idéologique des classes au Canada français," *Recherches sociographiques,* vol. 6, no. 1, January-April 1965, pp. 21-22. A publication of *Le département de sociologie et d'anthropologie,* Faculté des sciences sociales, Université Laval, Quebec.

8. Marcel Rioux, "Conscience ethnique et conscience de classe au Québec," *Recherches sociographiques,* vol. 6, no. 1, January-April 1965, pp. 31-32.

9. Jean-Réal Cardin, "Les nouveaux syndiqués," *Relations,* October 1966, no. 309, Montreal, p. 271.

10. Berque, *op. cit.,* p. 30.

11. Fernand Dumont, "Y a-t-il un avenir pour l'homme canadien français?" in *Le Devoir,* June 30, 1967.

10: The agonizing steps to freedom

1. Bernard Smith, "Le coup d'Etat du 29 avril." Montreal: Editions Actualité, 1970.
2. Robert Maheu, "Les francophones du Canada: 1941-1991," Editions Parti Pris, p. 11 (M.A. thesis for the Department of Demography, University of Montreal, 1968).
3. *Ibid.,* p. 73.
4. Henri Egretaud, "L'affaire Saint-Léonard." Montreal, 1970, p. 38.
5. Translator's note. CEGEP is the abbreviation of *Collège d'enseignement général et professionel;* the CEGEPs are post-secondary educational institutions somewhat like community colleges.
6. Through progressive revision of the electoral map, these districts, twelve in 1867, now number seventeen.
7. Smith, *op. cit.,* p. 35.
8. Newspaper of the English-speaking suburbs to the west of Montreal.
9. English newspapers in Montreal.
10. Initials of Pierre-Elliott Trudeau.
11. Translator's note. *Pieds noirs,* literally "black feet": a term of the popular language to describe French-speaking European colonists (mostly French) in North Africa.
12. See p. 177.
13. FRAP: "Les salariés au pouvoir." Montreal, 1970, p. 126.
14. Rodrigue Tremblay, *Indépendence et marché commun Québec-Etats-Unis.* Montreal: Editions du Jour, 1970.
15. *Le Devoir,* Montreal, November 14, 1970.

11: Quebec in transition

1. Translator's note. Mr. Rioux uses the terms "Canada" and "Canadian" to refer to Canada exclusive of Quebec.
2. François Meyer, *La surchauffe de la croissance (The Overheating of Growth).* Paris: Fayard, 1974.
3. The film, *Pour la suite du monde (Moontrap,* in English), is about a community at Isles-aux-coudres in the St. Lawrence which decided to revive an ancestral method of fishing.
4. An example of the type is Robert Bourassa, the former premier of Quebec. Shortly before his defeat by the *Parti québécois,* Bourassa repeatedly made vague statements in support of national goals in a futile attempt to win over the electorate.
5. F. Meyer, *op. cit.,* 123.

12: The end of innocence?

1.   In Chapter 11 we tried to identify those processes which underlie the recent changes in Quebec society.

2.   See "Politics as a vocation," in *From Max Weber: Essays in Sociology*, H.H. Gerth and C. Wright Mills, trans. and ed., New York: Oxford University Press, 1958.

3.   According to a recent report in the Paris newspaper *Le Monde*.

4.   At the present time, the groups in Canada and the United States that want to build a new social order are politically insignificant.

5.   See the "Rapport du tribunal de la culture" (Report of the Tribunal of Culture), *Liberté*, no. 101, 1975.

6.   In La Fontaine's *Fables* VII, 1, "The Animals Sick of the Plague," the lion calls a meeting of all the animals, who are suffering from a plague. He tells them that the plague is a punishment for their sins and suggests that the most sinful of the animals be punished, to win a general pardon. The lion and the other powerful animals are exonerated for their crimes, but when the meek donkey confesses that he has eaten a bit of grass from a monastery meadow, all the animals cry that he must be put on trial for this terrible deed, and the donkey is condemned to death.

7.   See above, p.110 and n.16.